budgetbooks

COUNTRY SONGS

ISBN 978-1-4584-0275-2

HAL•LEONARD®
CORPORATION

7777 W. BLUEMOUND RD. P.O. BOX 13819 MILWAUKEE, WI 53213

Visit Hal Leonard Online at
www.halleonard.com

CONTENTS

ABILENE

Words and Music by LESTER BROWN,
JOHN D. LOUDERMILK and BOB GIBSON

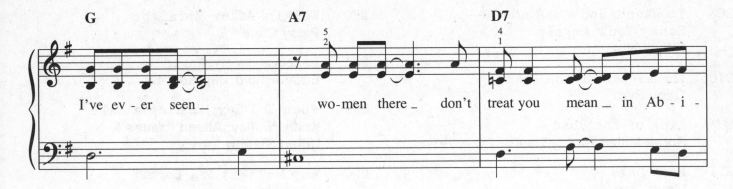

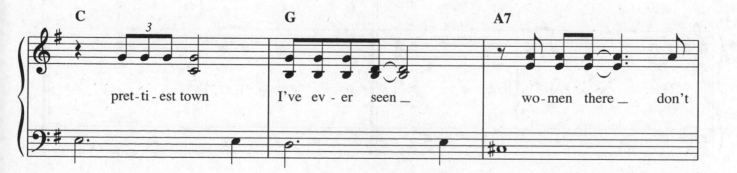

treat you mean — in Ab - i - lene, my Ab - i - lene.

Crowd-ed cit - y there ain't noth-ing free noth-ing in this

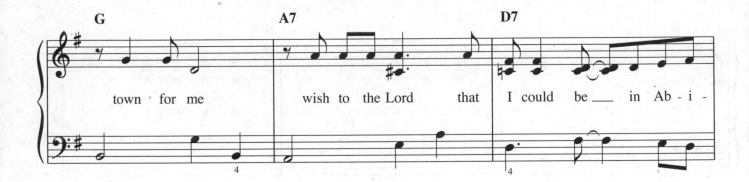

town for me wish to the Lord that I could be — in Ab - i -

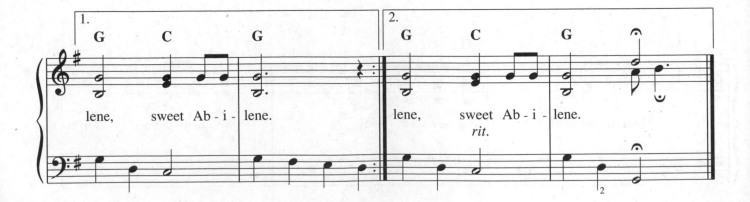

1.
lene, sweet Ab - i - lene.

2.
lene, sweet Ab - i - lene.
rit.

AIN'T GOIN' DOWN
('Til the Sun Comes Up)

Words and Music by KIM WILLIAMS,
GARTH BROOKS and KENT BLAZY

Bright Country

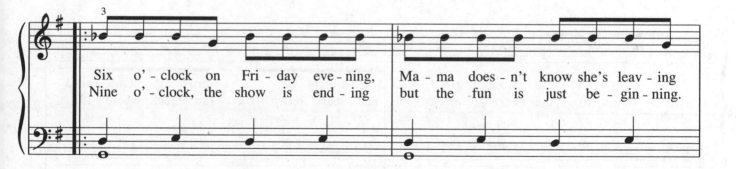

Six o'-clock on Fri-day eve-ning, Ma-ma does-n't know she's leav-ing
Nine o'-clock, the show is end-ing but the fun is just be-gin-ning.

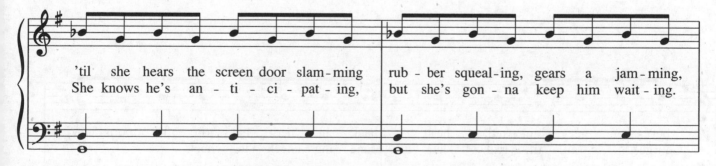

'til she hears the screen door slam-ming, rub-ber squeal-ing, gears a jam-ming,
She knows he's an-ti-ci-pat-ing, but she's gon-na keep him wait-ing.

8

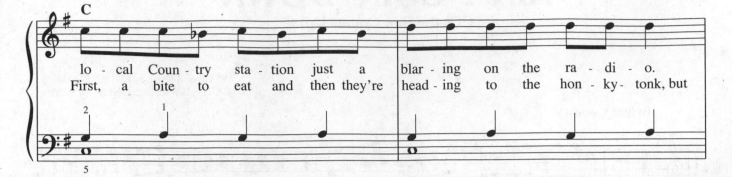

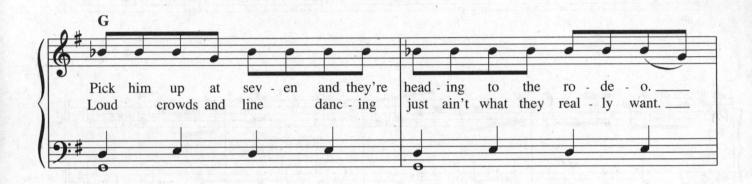

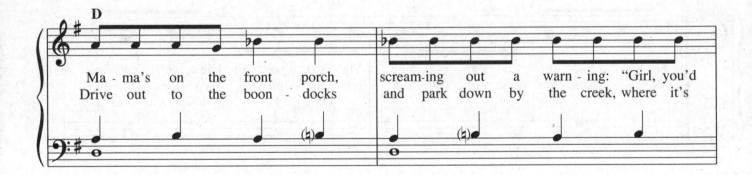

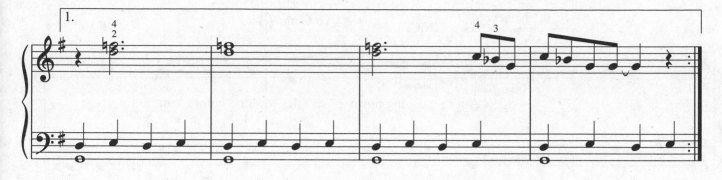

They ain't go - ing down 'til the

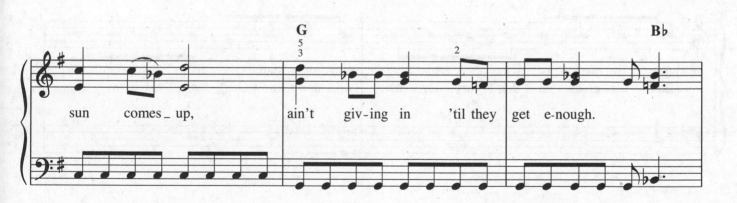

sun comes_ up, ain't giv-ing in 'til they get e-nough.

Go - ing 'round the world in a pick - up truck._____

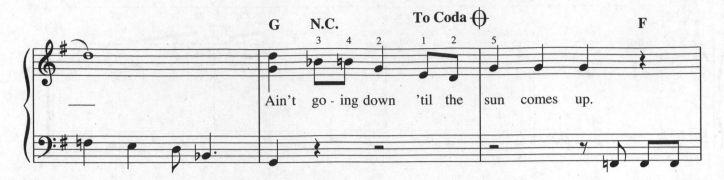

Ain't go-ing down 'til the sun comes up.

Ten 'til twelve is wine and danc-ing. Mid-night starts the hard ro-man-cing.
Six o'-clock on Sat-ur-day, her Folks don't know he's on his way. The

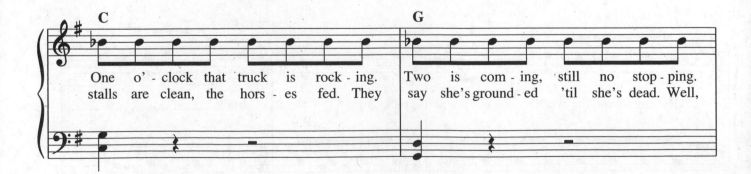

One o'-clock that truck is rock-ing. Two is com-ing, still no stop-ping.
stalls are clean, the hors-es fed. They say she's ground-ed 'til she's dead. Well,

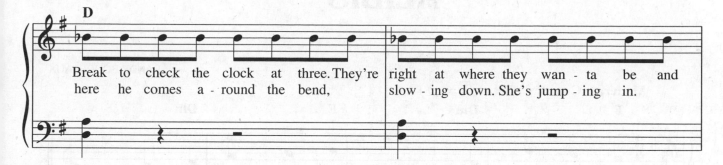

Break to check the clock at three. They're right at where they wan-ta be and
here he comes a-round the bend, slow-ing down. She's jump-ing in.

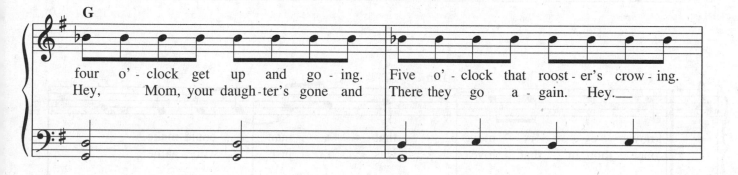

four o'-clock get up and go-ing. Five o'-clock that roost-er's crow-ing.
Hey, Mom, your daugh-ter's gone and There they go a-gain. Hey.___

1.
Hey. Yeah, they

CODA

2.
D.S. al Coda
They

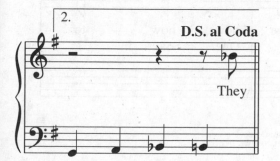
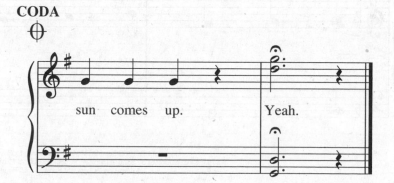

sun comes up. Yeah.

ALIBIS

Words and Music by
RANDY BOUDREAUX

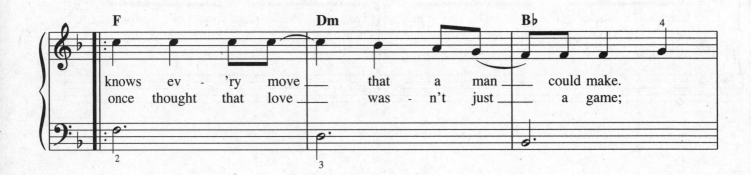

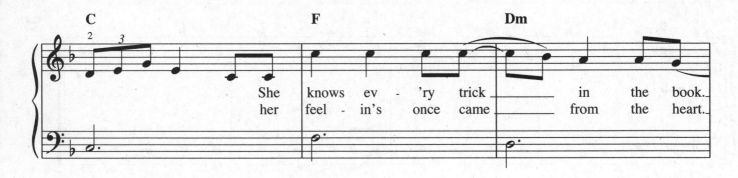

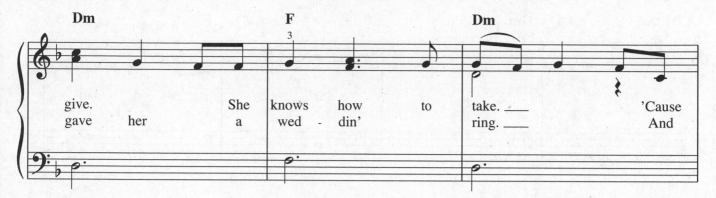

give. She knows how to take. ___ 'Cause
gave her a wed - din' ring. ___ And

so man - y times ___ she's been tak - en and fooled.
one night I tore ___ all those feel - in's a - part ___

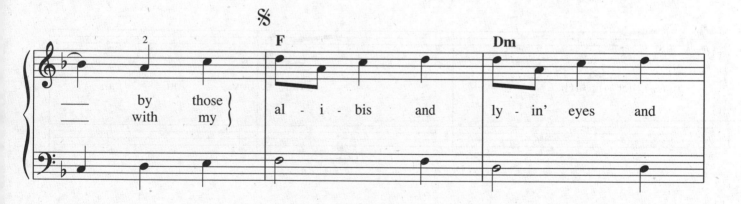

___ by those ⎫ al - i - bis and ly - in' eyes and
with my ⎭

all the best lines. Lord ___ knows she's heard 'em all.

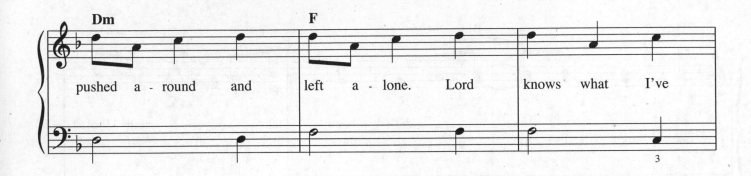

She's been cheat-ed on and pushed a-round and left a-lone. Lord knows what I've

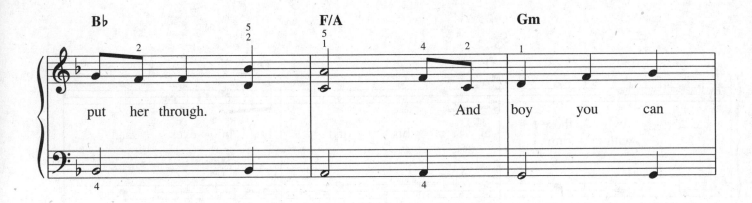

put her through. And boy you can

bet ____ if a move can be made, ____ she

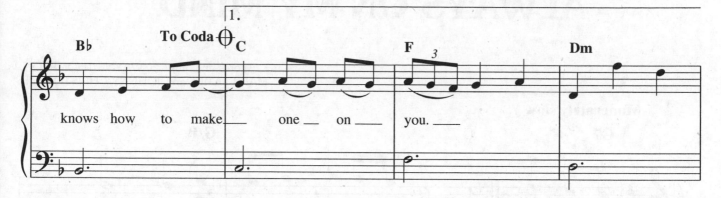

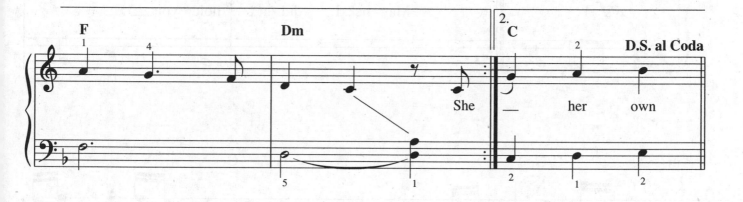

ALWAYS ON MY MIND

Words and Music by WAYNE THOMPSON,
MARK JAMES and JOHNNY CHRISTOPHER

Moderately slow

May-be I did-n't treat you _____
May-be I did-n't hold you _____

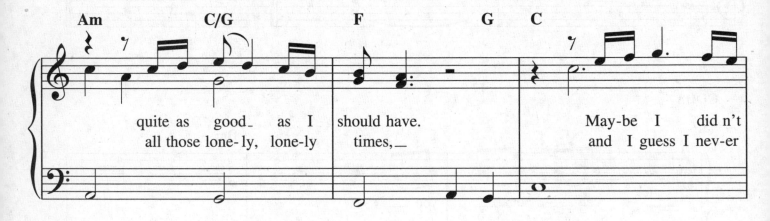

quite as good_ as I should have. May-be I did n't
all those lone-ly, lone-ly times,_ and I guess I nev-er

love you _____ quite as of-ten as I could have.
told you _____ I'm so hap-py that you're mine._

(1.,3.) Lit - tle things I should have said____ and done,
(2.) If I make you feel sec - ond best,

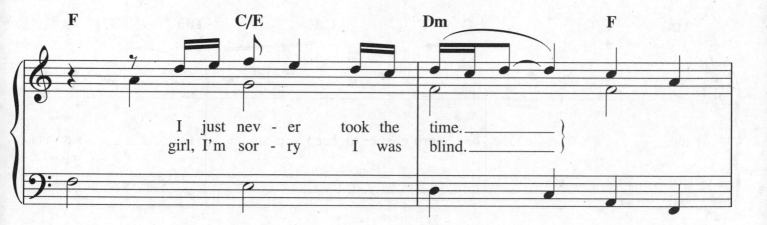

I just nev - er took the time.____
girl, I'm sor - ry I was blind.____

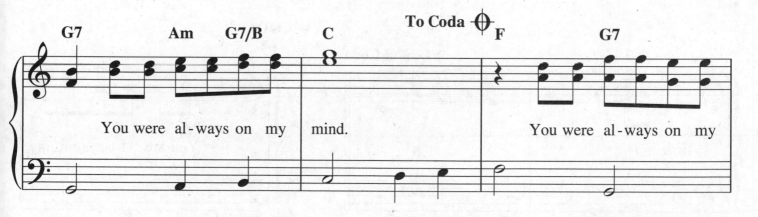

You were al-ways on my mind.

You were al-ways on my

To Coda

1. mind.

2. mind.

Tell____ me,

tell me that your sweet love— has n't died._____ Give_____

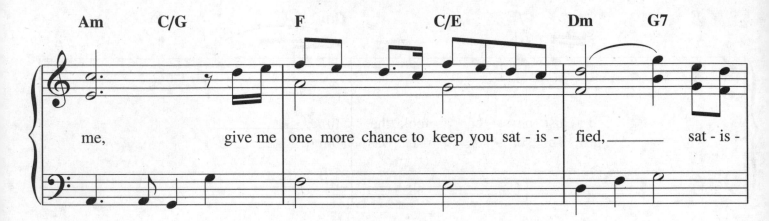

me, give me one more chance to keep you sat - is - fied,_____ sat - is -

D.S. al Coda

CODA

fied. You are al-ways on my

mind._____ You are al-ways on my mind.

rall.

AMAZED

Words and Music by MARV GREEN,
CHRIS LINDSEY and AIMEE MAYO

Moderately slow Country Ballad

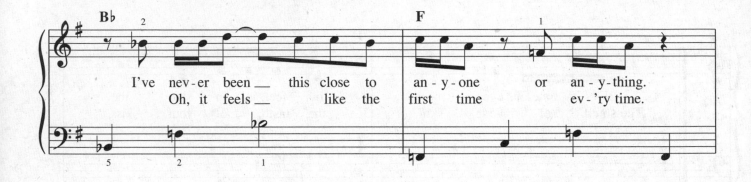

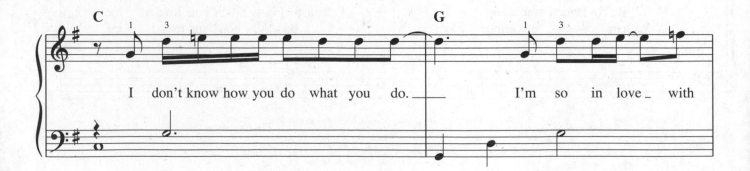

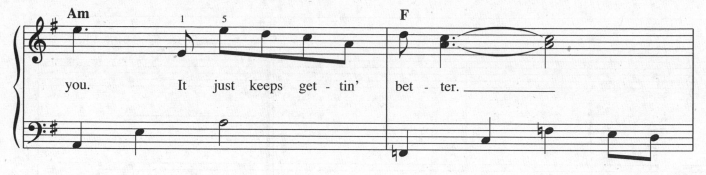

you. It just keeps get - tin' bet - ter. _____

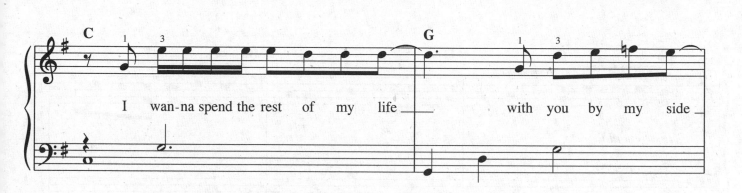

I wan-na spend the rest of my life _____ with you by my side ___

_____ for - ev - er and ev - er. _____

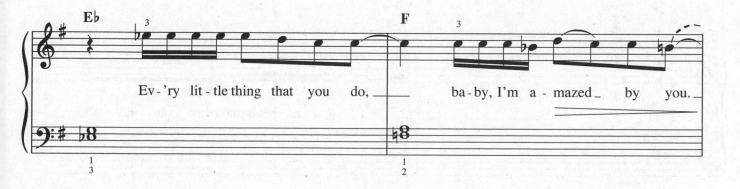

Ev -'ry lit - tle thing that you do, _____ ba - by, I'm a - mazed ___ by you. __

Instrumental

Ev-'ry lit-tle thing that you do.___ I'm so in love with you.___ It just keeps get-tin'

bet - ter.___ I wan-na spend the rest of my life___

with you by my side___ for - ev - er and ___ ev - er.

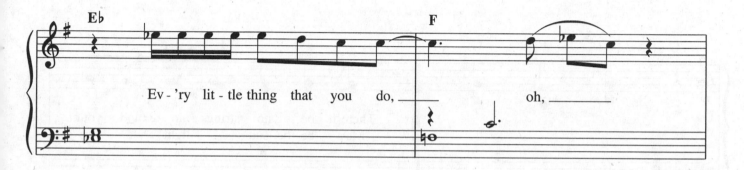

Ev - 'ry lit - tle thing that you do, ___ oh, ___

ev - 'ry lit - tle thing that you _ do, ___ ba - by, I'm a - mazed _ by ___

you.

ANGEL OF THE MORNING

Words and Music by
CHIP TAYLOR

Moderately slow, with a beat

There'll be no strings to bind your
May - be the sun's __ light will be

hands, not if my love can't bind your heart.
dim, and it won't mat - ter an - y - how.

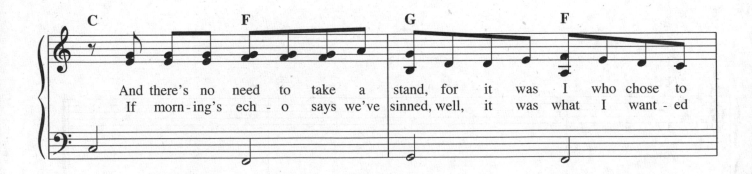

And there's no need to take a stand, for it was I who chose to
If morn - ing's ech - o says we've sinned, well, it was what I want - ed

start.
now.
I see no need to take me
And if we're vic-tims of the

home,
night,
I'm old e-nough to face the dawn.)
I won't be blind-ed by the light.)

mf Just call me An - gel ___ of the Morn - ing, (an - gel)

just touch my cheek be - fore you leave me, ba - by.

Just call me An - gel ___ of the Morn - ing, (an - gel)

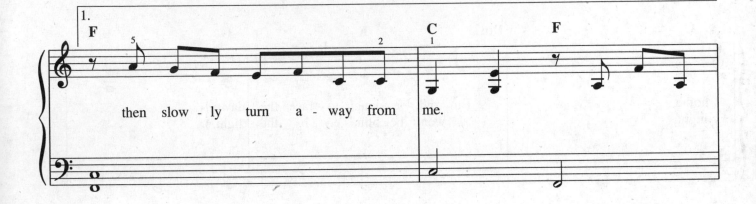

then slow - ly turn a - way from me.

then slow - ly turn a - way,

I won't beg you to stay with me, ___ through the

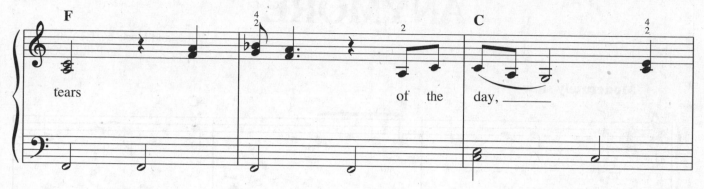

tears .... of the day, _____

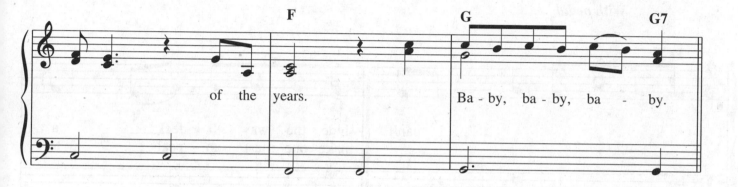

of the years. .... Ba - by, ba - by, ba - by.

Just call me An - gel _____ of the Morn - ing, (an - gel)

Repeat and Fade

just touch my cheek be - fore you leave me, ba - by.

ANYMORE

Words and Music by TRAVIS TRITT
and JILL COLUCCI

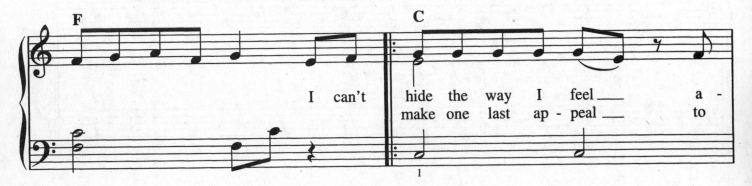

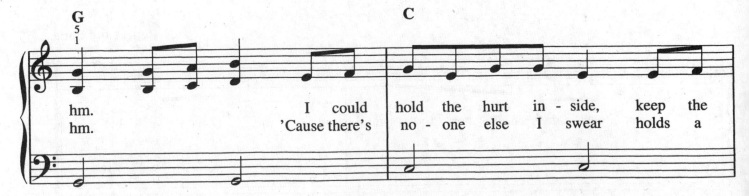

pain out of my eyes an - y - more. _____ Mm
can - dle an - y - where next to you. _____ Mm

hm.
hm.

My tears no long - er
My heart can't take the

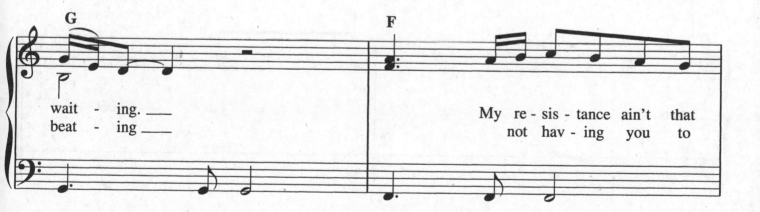

wait - ing. ___
beat - ing ___

My re - sis - tance ain't that
not hav - ing you to

strong.
hold.

My mind keeps re - cre -
A small voice keeps re -

at - ing _____ a love with you a - lone. _____ And I'm
peat-ing _____ deep in - side my soul. _____ It says I

tired of pre - tend - ing ___ I don't love you an - y -
can't keep pre - tend - ing ___ I don't love you an - y -

1.

more. Let me

2.

more. I've got to take the chance or ___

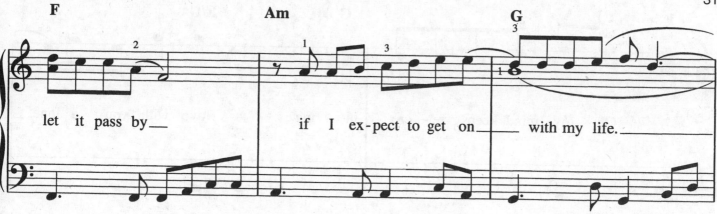

let it pass by ___   if I ex-pect to get on ___ with my life. ___

My tears no long-er

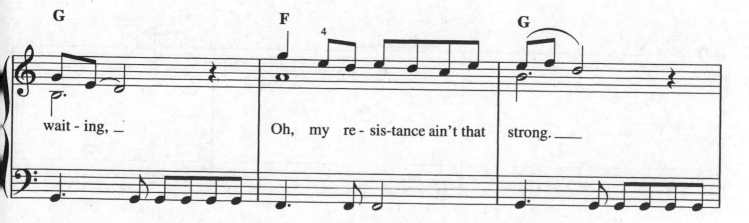

wait-ing, ___   Oh, my re-sis-tance ain't that   strong. ___

Oh, my mind keeps re - cre - at - ing a love with you a lone.

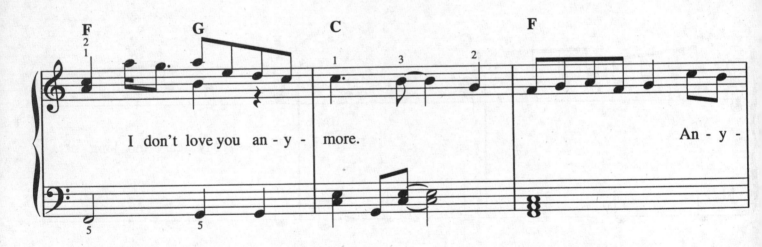

And I'm tired of pre - tend - ing

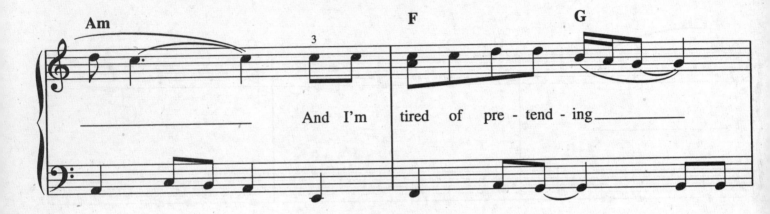

I don't love you an - y - more. An - y -

more. _ rit. An - y - more. _

BLESS THE BROKEN ROAD

Words and Music by MARCUS HUMMON,
BOBBY BOYD and JEFF HANNA

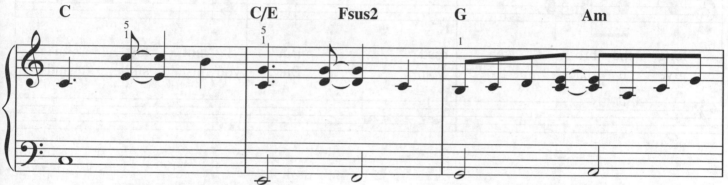

I set out___ on a
think a - bout___ the

nar - row way___ man - y years___ a - go,
years I've spent___ just pass - in' through. I'd

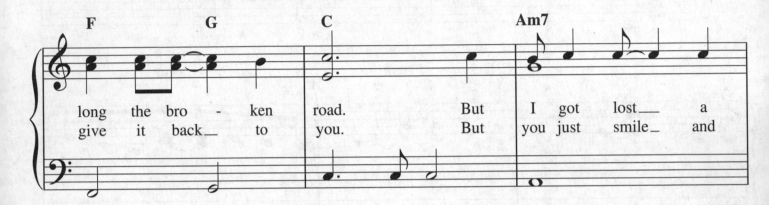

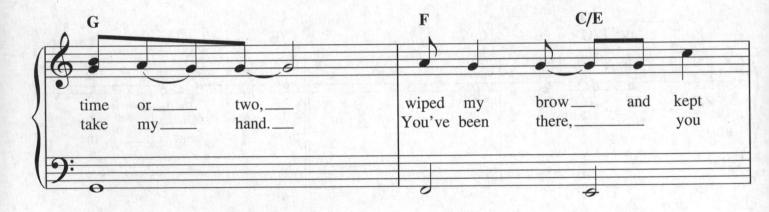

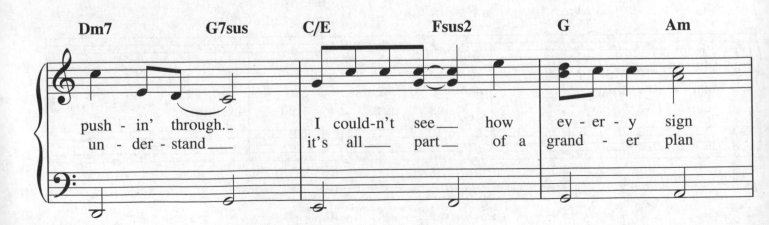

point - ed straight_ to you.
that is com - in' true. But ev - er - y
Ev - er - y

long lost_ dream_ led me to where you_ are._

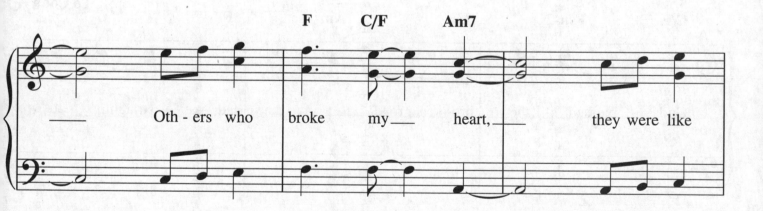

_ Oth - ers who broke my_ heart,_ they were like

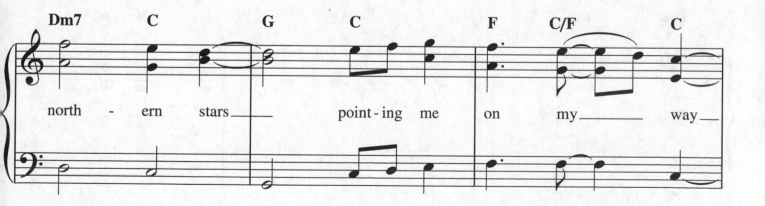

north - ern stars_ point - ing me on my_ way_

in - to your   lov - ing_____ arms._____   This much I

know_____ is_____   true: that

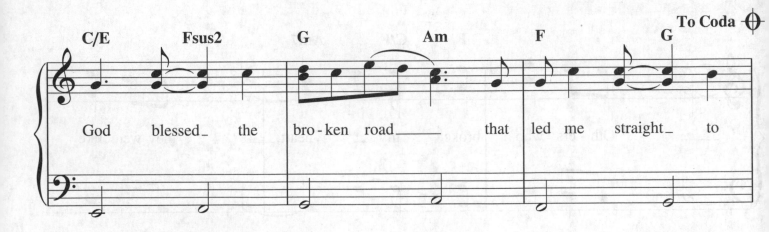

God   blessed_   the   bro - ken road_____   that   led me   straight_   to

you.

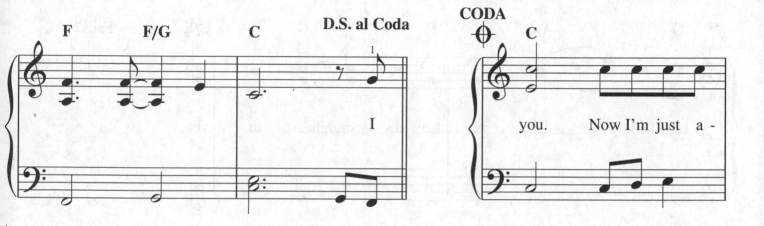

roll - in'___ home___ in - to my lov - er's____ arms.___

___ This much I know____ is____

true: that God blessed_ the

bro - ken road_____ that led me straight_ to you,

that God blessed_ the   bro - ken

road _____ that led me straight_____

_____ to you.

rit.

BIG BAD JOHN

Words and Music by
JIMMY DEAN

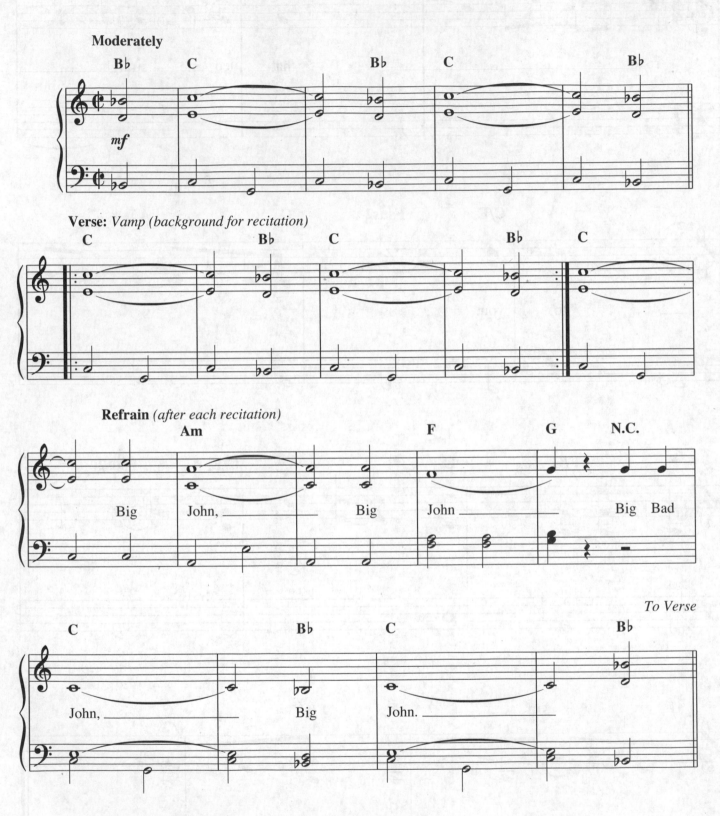

Recitation

Verse 1:   Every morning at the mine you could see him arrive,
He stood six-foot-six and weighed two-forty-five.
Kind of broad at the shoulder and narrow at the hip,
And everybody knew you didn't give no lip to Big John!
Refrain

Verse 2:   Nobody seemed to know where John called home,
He just drifted into town and stayed all alone.
He didn't say much, a-kinda quiet and shy,
And if you spoke at all, you just said, "Hi" to Big John!
Somebody said he came from New Orleans,
Where he got in a fight over a Cajun queen.
And a crashing blow from a huge right hand
Send a Louisiana fellow to the promised land. Big John!
Refrain

Verse 3:   Then came the day at the bottom of the mine
When a timber cracked and the men started crying.
Miners were praying and hearts beat fast,
And everybody thought that they'd breathed their last 'cept John.
Through the dust and the smoke of this man-made hell
Walked a giant of a man that the miners knew well.
Grabbed a sagging timber and gave out with a groan,
And, like a giant oak tree, just stood there alone. Big John!
Refrain

Verse 4:   And with all of his strength, he gave a mighty shove;
Then a miner yelled out, "There's a light up above!"
And twenty men scrambled from a would-be grave,
And now there's only one left down there to save; Big John!
With jacks and timbers they started back down
Then came that rumble way down in the ground,
And smoke and gas belched out of that mine,
Everybody knew it was the end of the line for Big John!
Refrain

Verse 5:   Now they never re-opened that worthless pit,
They just placed a marble stand in front of it;
These few words are written on that stand:
"At the bottom of this mine lies a big, big man: Big John!"
Refrain

BLUE

Words and Music by
BILL MACK

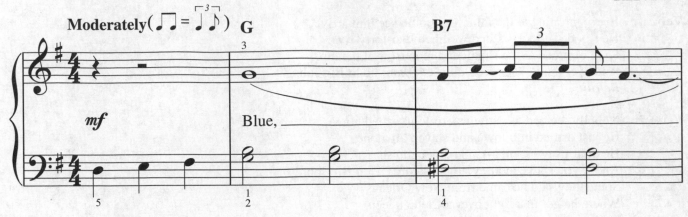

Blue, oh, so lone-some for you. Why can't you be

blue _____ o - ver me?

Blue, _____ oh, so
Instrumental solo

lone - some   for   you.   Tears   fill   my   eyes   'til   I   can't

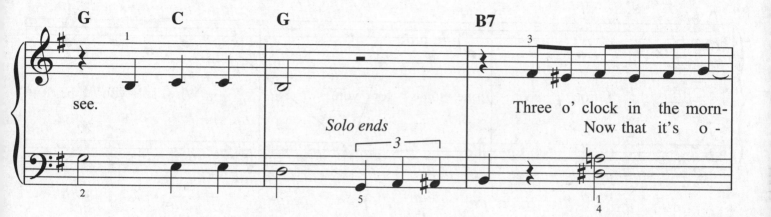

see.   *Solo ends*   Three o' clock in   the morn-
                                                           Now that it's   o -

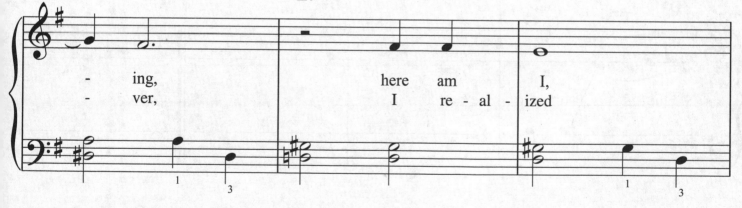

- ing,   here   am   I,
- ver,   I   re - al - ized

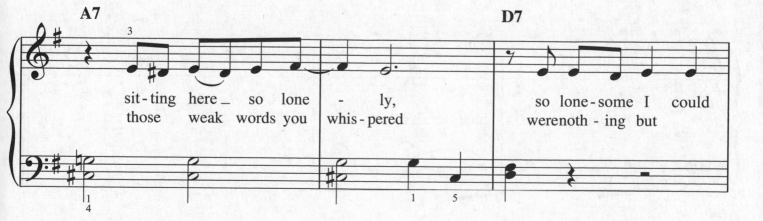

sit - ting   here _ so   lone - ly,   so lone - some I   could
those   weak words you   whis - pered   werenoth - ing   but

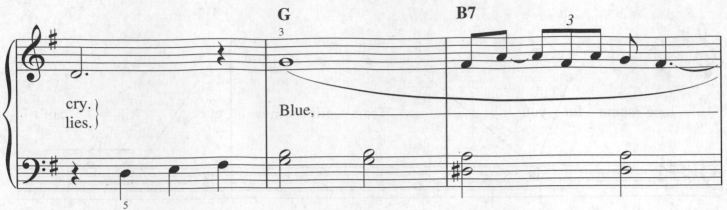

cry.
lies.

Blue,

oh, so lone-some for you.

Why can't you be

blue ____ o - ver me?

me?

Why can't you be blue ____ o - ver me?

BLUE EYES CRYING IN THE RAIN

Words and Music by
FRED ROSE

In the twi - light glow I see her
Now my hair has turned to sil - ver

blue eyes cry - ing in the
all my life I've loved in

rain. _____
vain. _____

As I we can

kissed good - bye and part - ed
see her star in heav - en

C7   **F**   **Bb**

knew we'd nev - er meet a - gain.
blue eyes cry - ing in the rain.

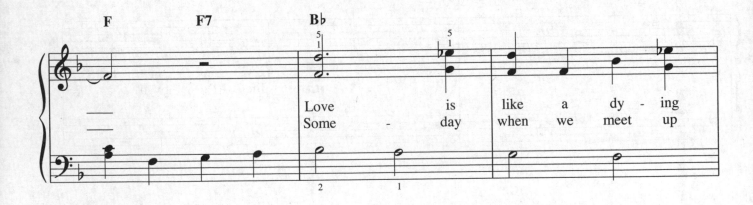

F   **F7**   **Bb**

Love is like a dy - ing
Some - day when we meet up

em - ber   **F**   on - ly
yon - der   we'll stroll

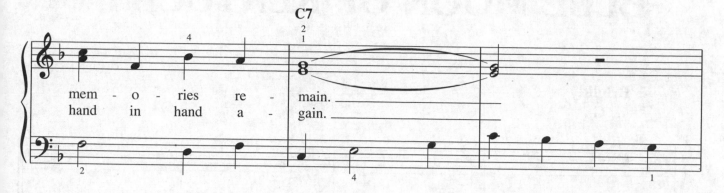

C7

mem – o – ries re – main. _____
hand in hand a – gain. _____

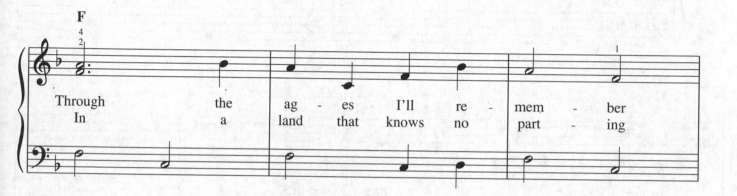

F

Through the ag – es I'll re – mem – ber
In a land that knows no part – ing

C7

blue eyes cry – ing in the
blue eyes cry – ing in the

1.
F   B♭   F

rain. _____

2.
F   B♭   F

rain. _____

BLUE MOON OF KENTUCKY

Words and Music by
BILL MONROE

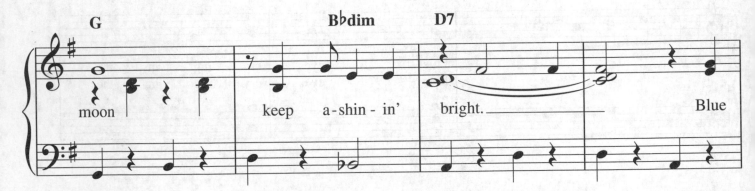

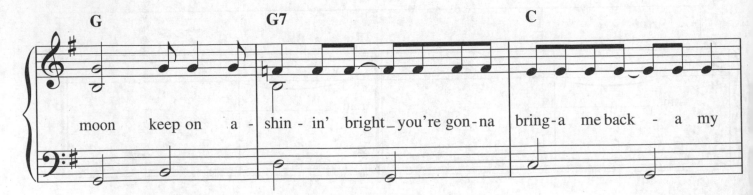

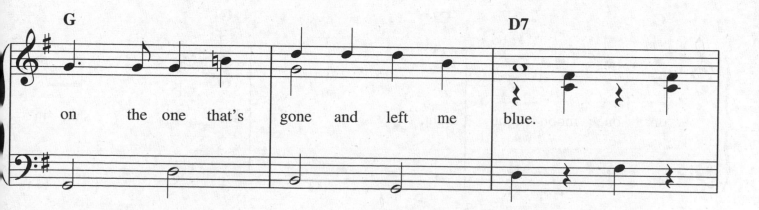

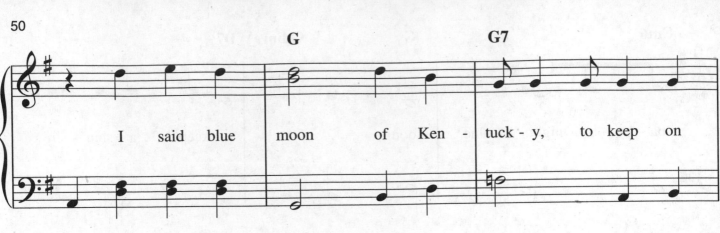

I said blue moon of Ken - tuck - y, to keep on

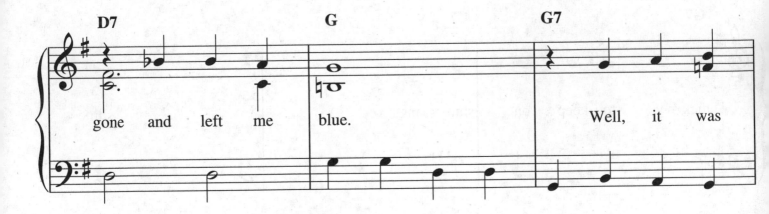

shin - ing, shine on the one that's

gone and left me blue. Well, it was

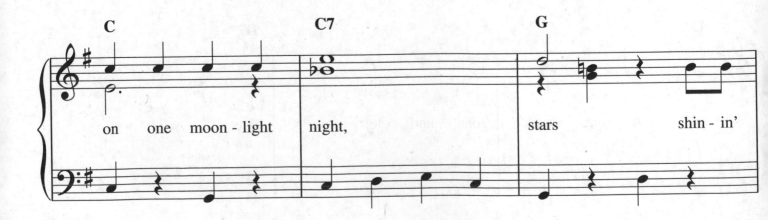

on one moon - light night, stars shin - in'

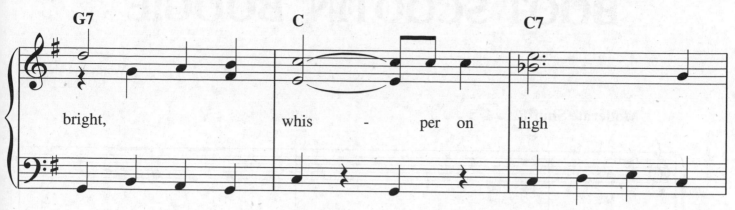

bright,   whis - per on   high

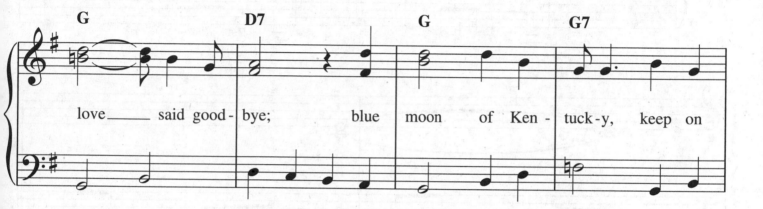

love___ said good - bye;   blue   moon   of Ken - tuck-y,   keep on

shin - ing,   shine   on   the one that's   gone and   left__ me

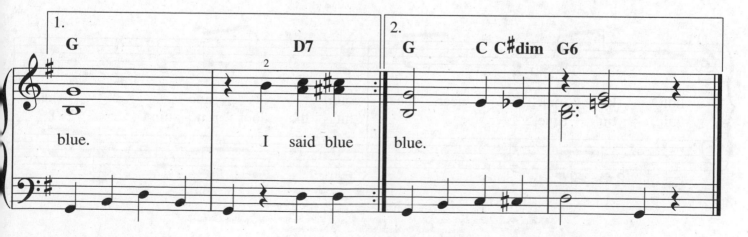

1. blue.   I   said blue   **2.** blue.

BOOT SCOOTIN' BOOGIE

Words and Music by
RONNIE DUNN

1. Out in the coun-try past the cit-y lim-it sign,___ well there's a
2. got a good job, I work hard for my money. When it's
3. *Instrumental*
4. *(See additional lyrics)*

hon-ky tonk___ near the coun-ty line.___ The
quit-tin' time,___ I hit the door run-nin'. I

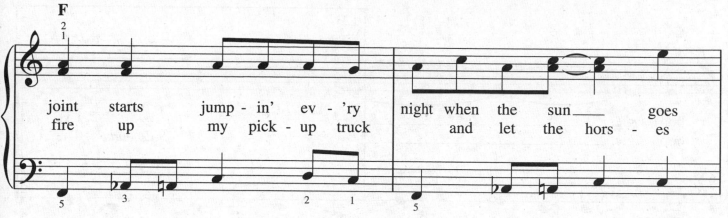

F

joint   starts   jump - in'   ev - 'ry   night   when   the   sun____   goes
fire   up   my   pick - up   truck   and   let   the   hors - es

C

down.____   They   got
run.____   I   go

G

whis - key,   wom - en,____   mu - sic   and   smoke.   It's
fly - in' down   that high - way   to   that   hide - a - way

where   all   the   cow - boy   folk   go   to   boot   scoot - in'
stuck   out   in   the   woods,   to   do   the   boot   scoot - in'

54

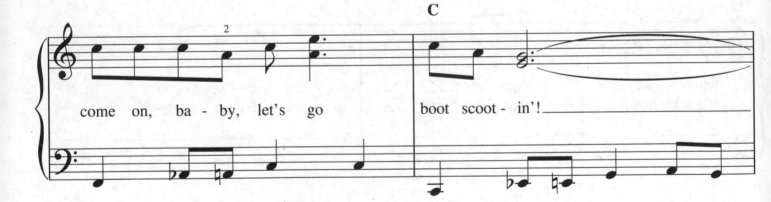

ba - by, meet me out back, we're gon - na boo - gie.

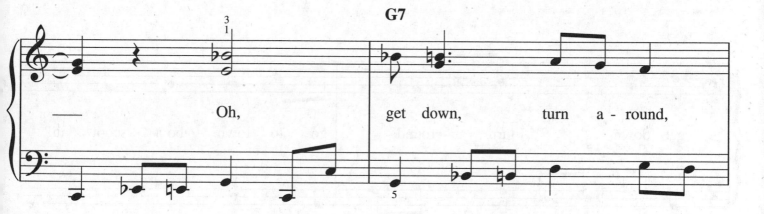

Oh, get down, turn a - round,

go to town, boot scoot-in' boo - gie.

Whoa, I said get down, turn a-round,

go to town,   boot scoot-in' |boo - gie._____   Whoa,

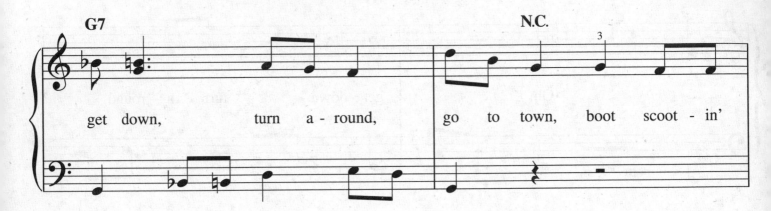

get down,   turn a - round,   go to town, boot scoot - in'

boo - gie._____

Additional Lyrics

4. The bartender asks me, says,
   "Son, what will it be?"
   I want a shot at that redhead yonder lookin' at me.
   The dance floor's hoppin'
   And it's hotter than the Fourth of July.
   I see outlaws, inlaws, crooks and straights
   All out makin' it shake doin' the boot scootin' boogie.
   Chorus

BREATHE

Words and Music by HOLLY LAMAR
and STEPHANIE BENTLEY

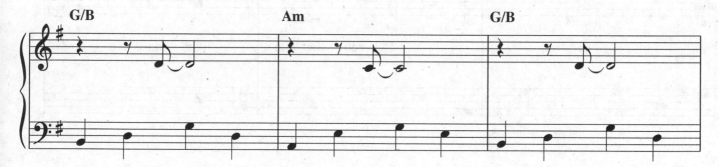

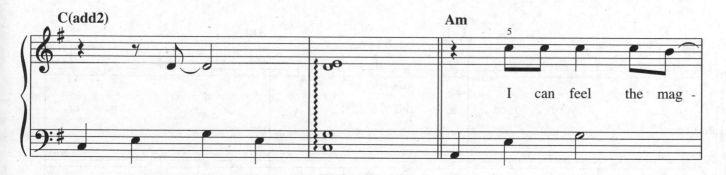

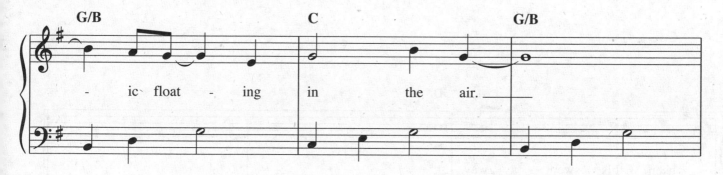

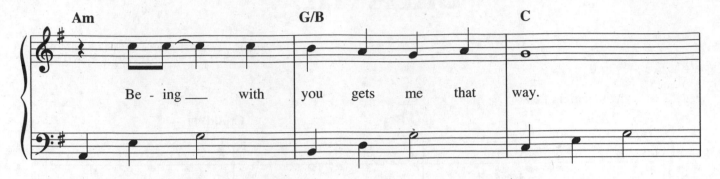

Be - ing___ with you gets me that way.

I watch the sun - light dance a - cross___

___ your face___ and I ___ nev - er

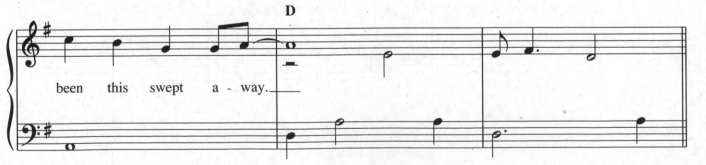

been this swept a - way.___

All my thoughts just seem to set - tle on the breeze
In a way I know my heart _ is wak - ing up _

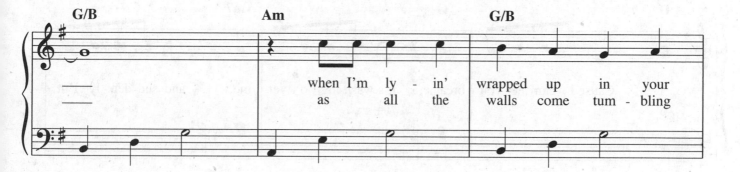

_
_
when I'm ly - in' wrapped up in your
as all the walls come tum - bling

arms. The whole world just
down. Clos-er than I've

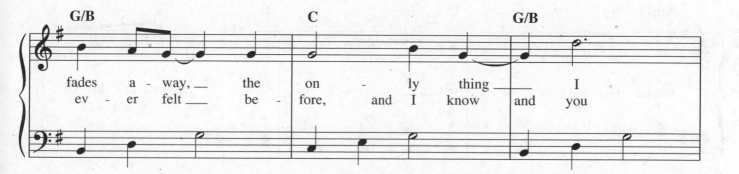

fades a - way, _ the on - ly thing _ I
ev - er felt _ be - fore, and I know and you

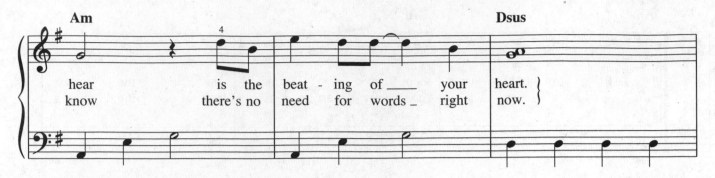

Am ... Dsus

hear   is the   beat - ing of ____ your   heart.
know   there's no   need   for   words _ right   now.

D ... G ... Am7

'Cause I can feel you   breathe,   it's wash-ing o - ver   me,   and sud-den - ly I'm

C ... D ... G

melt - ing in - to you. ___ There's noth-ing left to   prove,   ba - by, all we

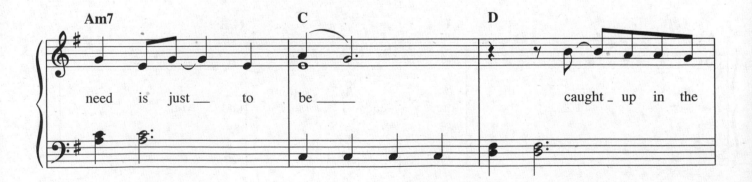

Am7 ... C ... D

need   is   just _ to   be ____   caught _ up in the

touch, the slow and stead - y rush. Ba - by, is - n't that the way__ that

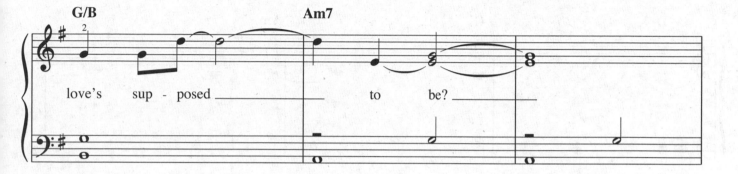

love's sup - posed _____ to be? _____

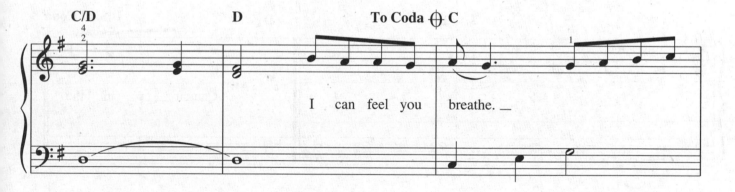

I can feel you breathe. __

Just

breathe.

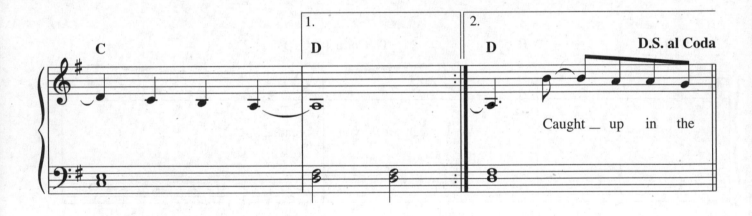

Caught _ up in the

CODA

breathe. _

Just _____ breathe.

I can feel the mag -

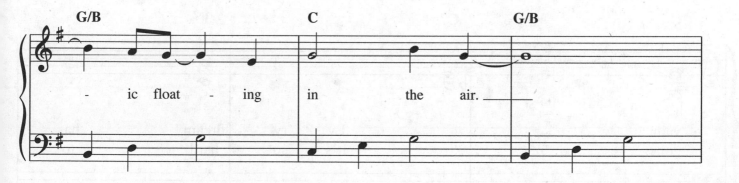

- ic float - ing in the air. _____

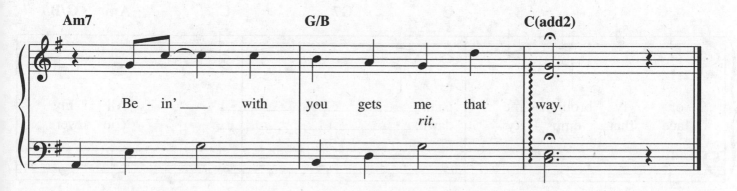

Be - in' _____ with you gets me that way.

rit.

BORN TO LOSE

Words and Music by
TED DAFFAN

Moderately, in 2

Born to lose, I've lived my life in
lose, my ev - 'ry hope is

vain. Ev - 'ry dream has to
gone. It's so hard

on - ly brought me pain. All my
face that emp - ty dawn. You were

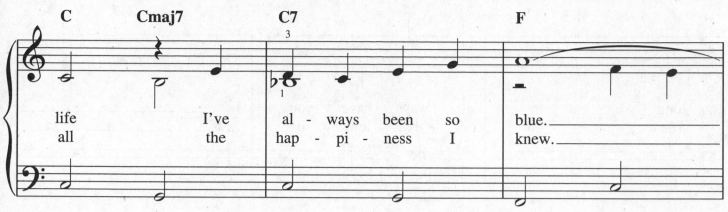

life I've al - ways been so blue.
all the hap - pi - ness I knew.

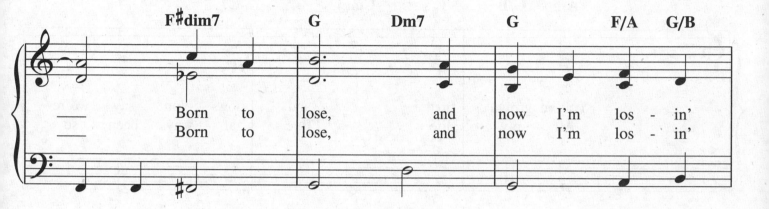

Born to lose, and now I'm los - in'
Born to lose, and now I'm los - in'

you. Born to lose, it
you. There's no use to

seems so hard to bear, how I
dream of hap - pi - ness, all I

long to al - ways have you near.____
see is on - ly lone - li - ness.____

____ You've grown tired and now you say we're
____ All my life I've al - ways been so

through.____ Born to lose, and
blue.____

now I'm los - in' you.____ Born to

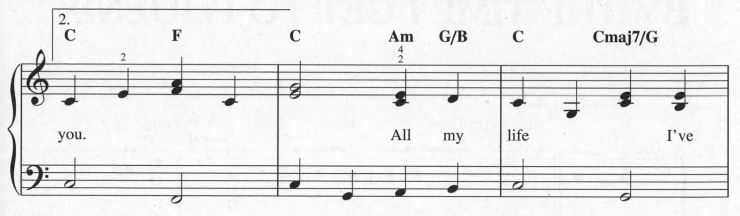

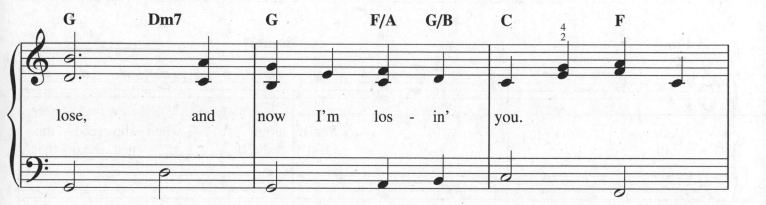

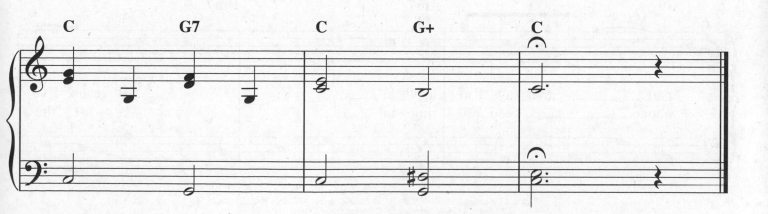

BY THE TIME I GET TO PHOENIX

Words and Music by
JIMMY WEBB

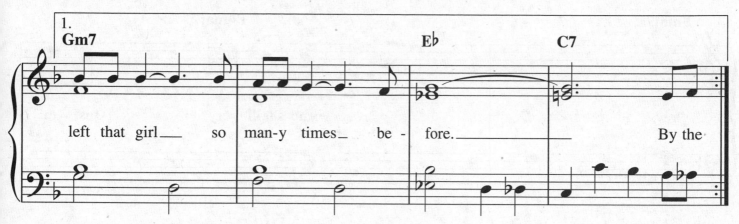

1.
left that girl___ so man-y times___ be - fore.___ By the

2.
wall, that's all.___ By the

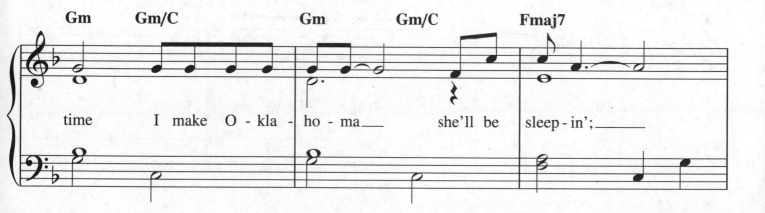

time I make O - kla - ho - ma___ she'll be sleep-in';___

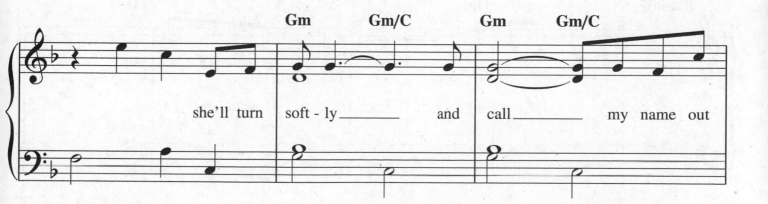

she'll turn soft - ly___ and call___ my name out

low.　　　　　　　　　　　And she'll　cry　　　　just　to

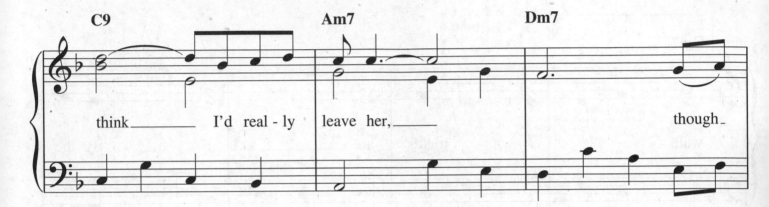

think＿＿＿　I'd real - ly　leave her,＿＿＿　　　　　though＿

time　and　time＿＿＿　　I've tried＿　to tell her　so;

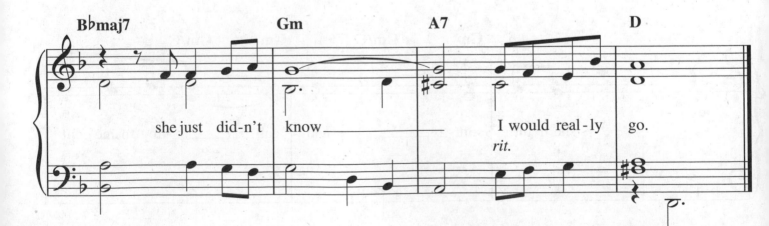

she just did-n't　know＿＿＿＿＿　　I would real - ly　go.
rit.

THE CHAIR

Words and Music by HANK COCHRAN
and DEAN DILLON

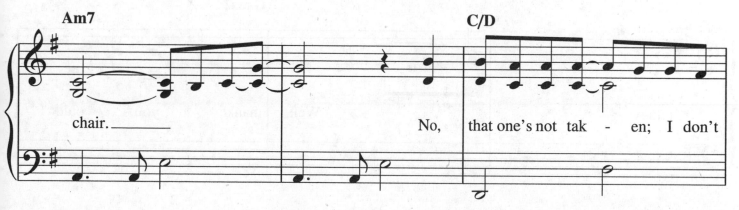

Well, ex - cuse me,___ but I think you've___ got my

chair._____ No, that one's not tak - en; I don't

mind if you sit here. I'll be glad to share.. Yeah, it's

u - sually ___ packed here on ___ Fri-day nights. ___

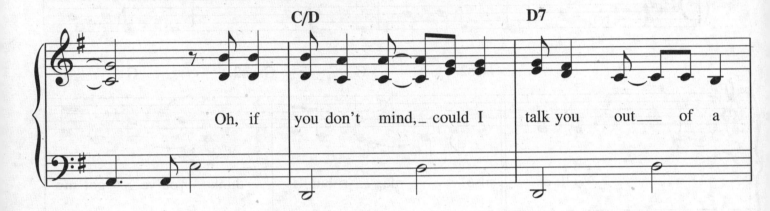

Oh, if you don't mind, ___ could I talk you out ___ of a

light? Well, thank you, ___ could I

drink you ___ a buy? Oh, lis - ten to me. ___ What I mean ___

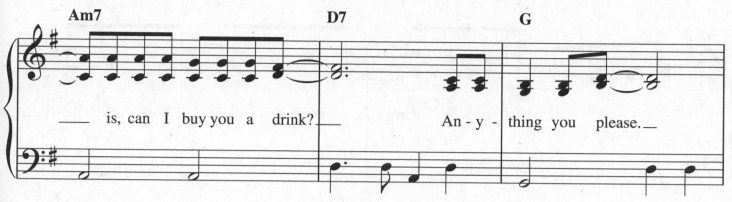

is, can I buy you a drink?___ An - y - thing you please.___

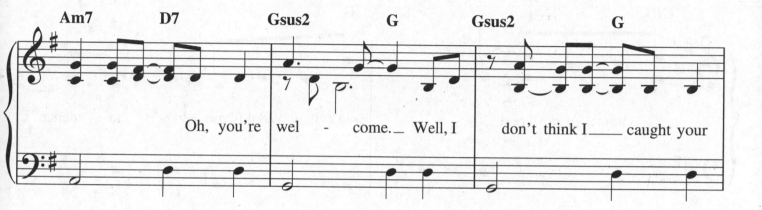

Oh, you're wel - come.___ Well, I don't think I___ caught your

name.___ Are you wait - ing for some - one to meet___

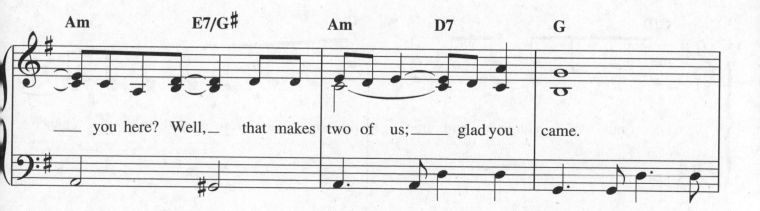

___ you here? Well,___ that makes two of us;___ glad you came.

74

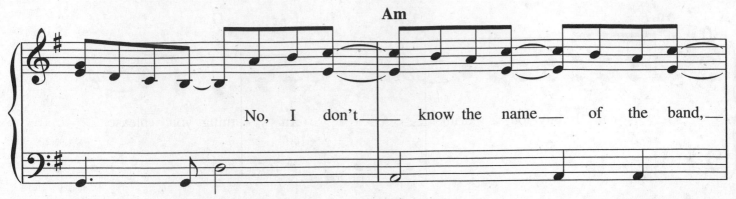

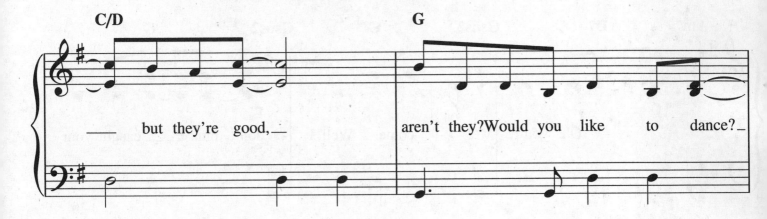

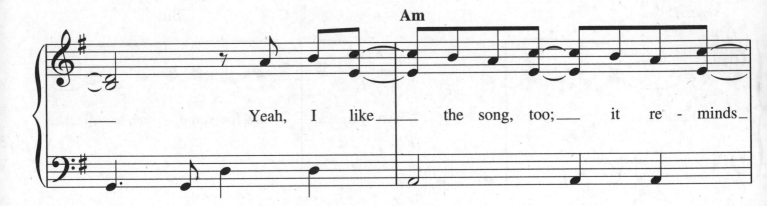

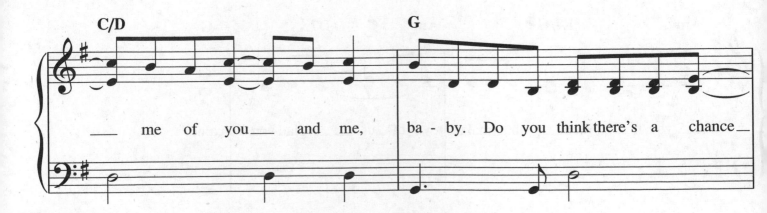

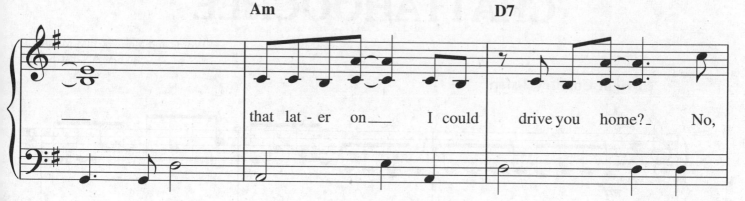

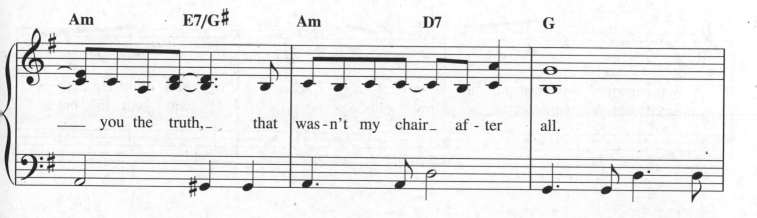

CHATTAHOOCHEE

Words and Music by JIM McBRIDE
and ALAN JACKSON

Bright Country 2-step

2. Well, we

1. Way down   yon-der on the   Chat-ta-hoo-chee   it   gets   hot-ter than a
fogged up the win dows in ___   my   old Chev-y;   I   was will-in' but ___

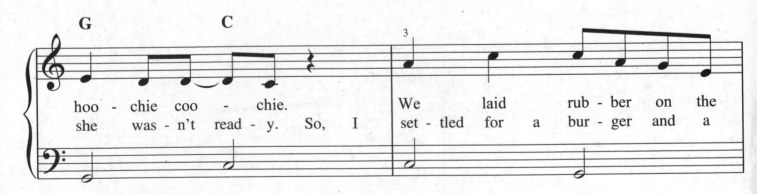

hoo-chie coo-chie.   We   laid   rub-ber on the
she was-n't read-y. So, I   set-tled for a   bur-ger and a

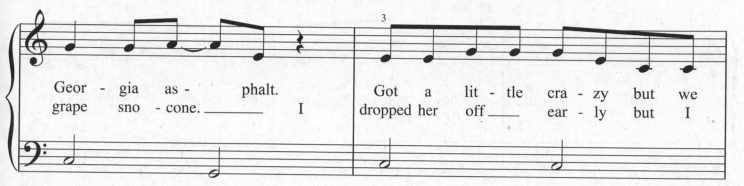

Geor - gia as - phalt.
grape sno - cone. _____ I

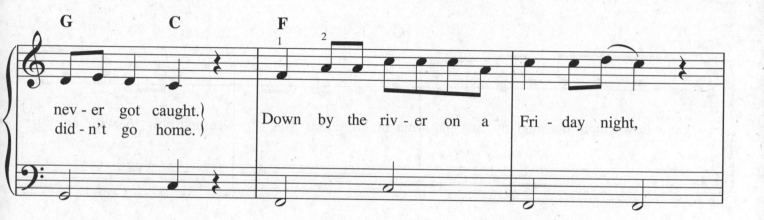

G   C
nev - er got caught.
did - n't go home.

F
Down by the riv - er on a   Fri - day night,

C
Pyr - a - mid of cans in the pale moon - light,

G   C
F
talk - ing 'bout cars and

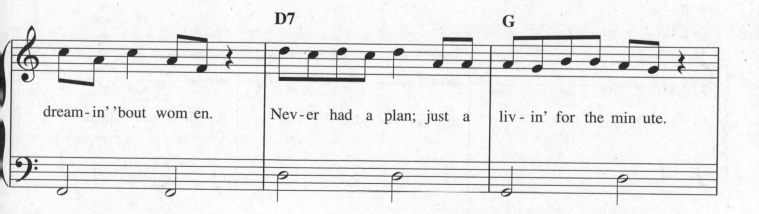

dream-in' 'bout wom en.

D7
Nev - er had a plan; just a

G
liv - in' for the min ute.

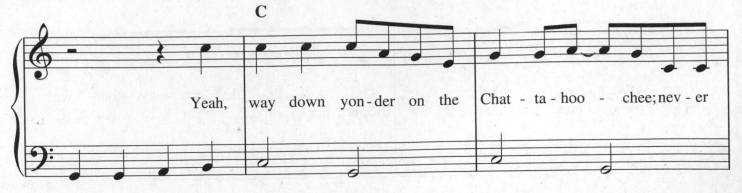

Yeah, way down yon-der on the Chat - ta - hoo - chee; nev - er

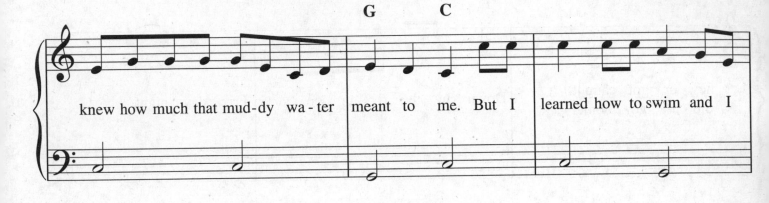

knew how much that mud-dy wa - ter meant to me. But I learned how to swim and I

1.

learned who I was; a lot a-bout liv-in' and a lit - tle 'bout love.

2.

lit - tle 'bout love, a lot a-bout liv-in' and a lit - tle 'bout _ love.

rit.

CRYIN' TIME

Words and Music by
BUCK OWENS

lived to be a hun-dred years old. Oh, it's cry-in' time a-gain, you're gon-na

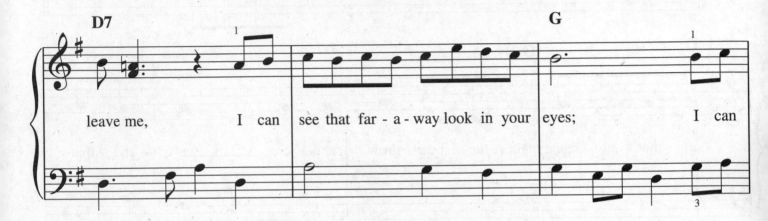

leave me, I can see that far - a - way look in your eyes; I can

tell by the way you hold me dar - lin' that it

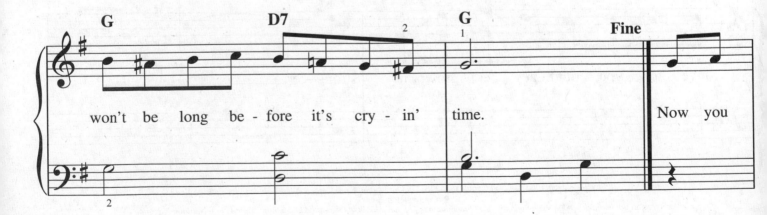

won't be long be - fore it's cry - in' time. Now you

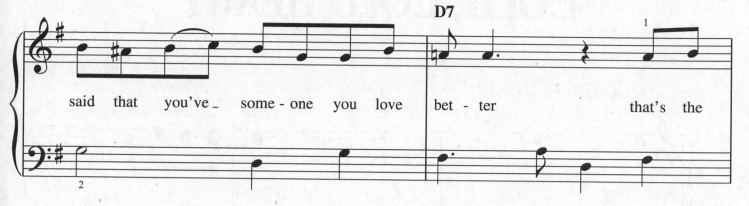

said that you've_ some-one you love bet - ter that's the

D7

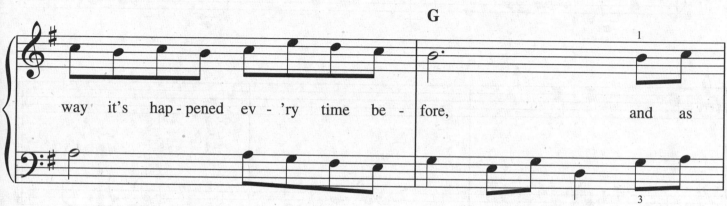

way it's hap-pened ev - 'ry time be - fore, and as

G

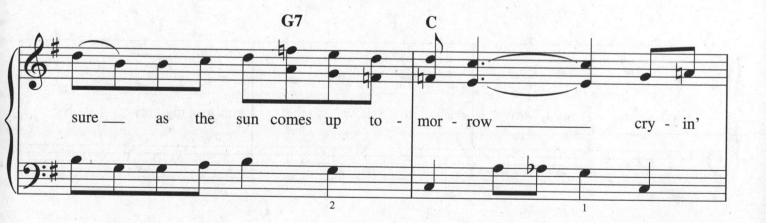

sure ___ as the sun comes up to - mor - row _____ cry - in'

G7   **C**

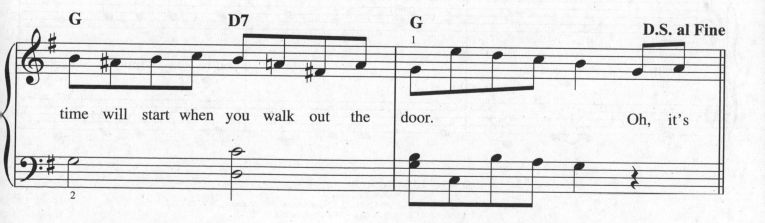

time will start when you walk out the door. Oh, it's

G   **D7**   **G**   **D.S. al Fine**

COLD, COLD HEART

Words and Music by
HANK WILLIAMS

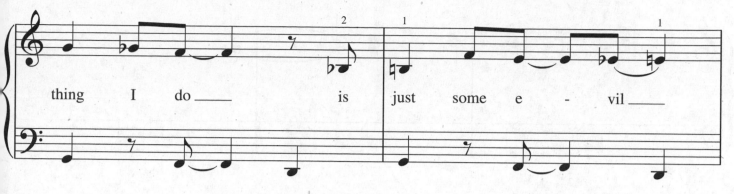

thing   I   do ____   is   just   some   e - vil ____

scheme.   A mem -'ry from your   lone - some past __

keeps us   so __ far a - part.   Why   can't   I   free __   your

doubt - ful mind __   and melt your cold, cold   heart? _____

An -

oth - er love ___ be - fore my time ___ made

G7

your heart ___ sad and blue, and

so my heart is pay - ing now ___ for things I ___ did - n't ___

In an - ger un - kind words I said

that made the tear-drops start. ___ Why can't I free ___ your

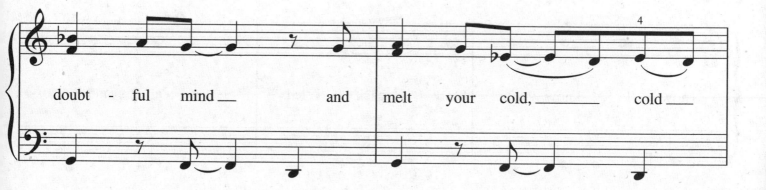

doubt - ful mind ___ and melt your cold, ___ cold ___

heart?

There was a time when I be - lieved _ that

G7

you be - longed _ to me, but

now I know your heart is shack - led to a __ mem - o -

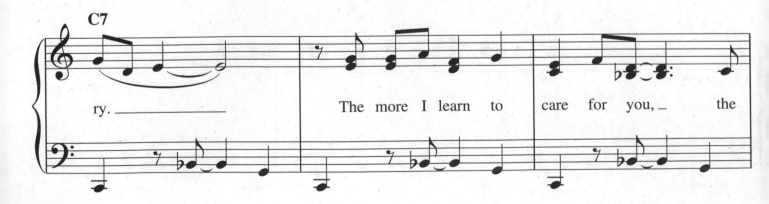

C7

ry. _____ The more I learn to care for you, _ the

more we drift a - part._____ Why can't I free_____

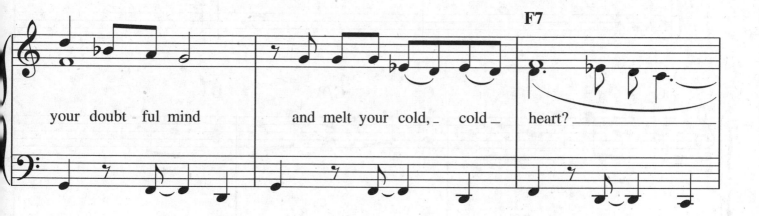

your doubt - ful mind and melt your cold,_ cold_ heart?_____

8vb ⌋

COWBOY TAKE ME AWAY

Words and Music by MARCUS HUMMON
and MARTIE SEIDEL

Moderately slow

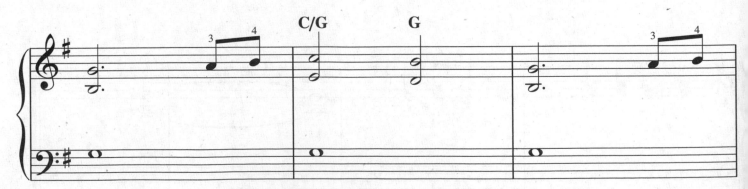

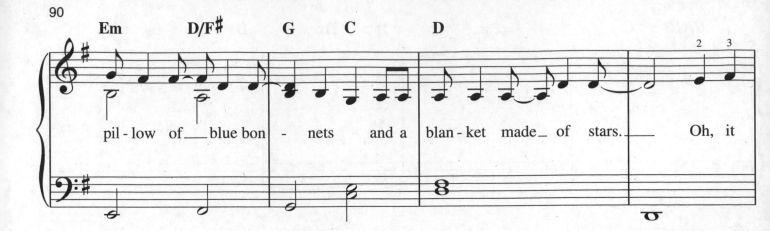

pil - low of ___ blue bon - nets and a blan - ket made ___ of stars. ___ Oh, it

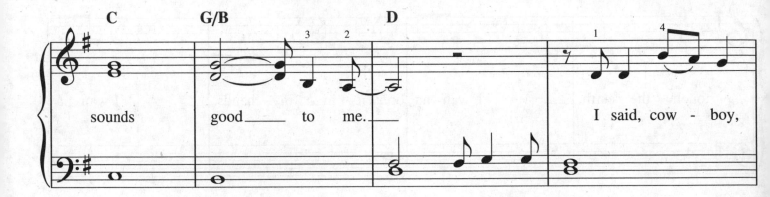

sounds good ___ to me. ___ I said, cow - boy,

take ___ me ___ a - way. ___ Fly this girl ___ as high ___

___ as you can ___ in - to the wild ___ blue. ___ Set ___ me

free,___ oh,___ I pray,___ clos - er___ to

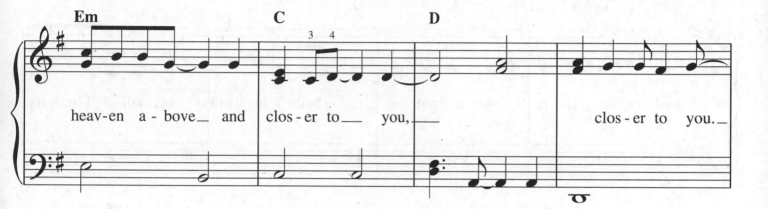

heav-en a - bove___ and clos - er to___ you,___ clos - er to you.___

I wan-na

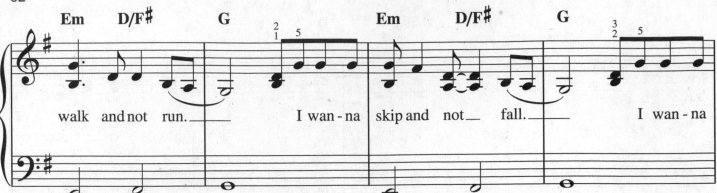

walk and not run. I wan-na skip and not__ fall.__ I wan-na

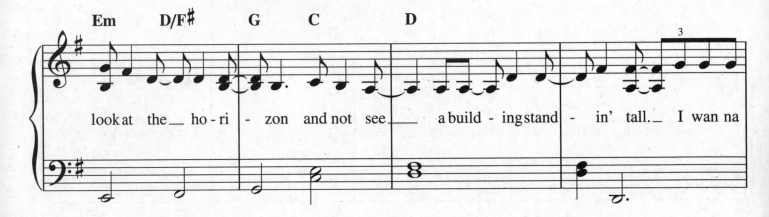

look at the__ ho - ri - zon and not see__ a build-ing stand - in' tall.__ I wan na

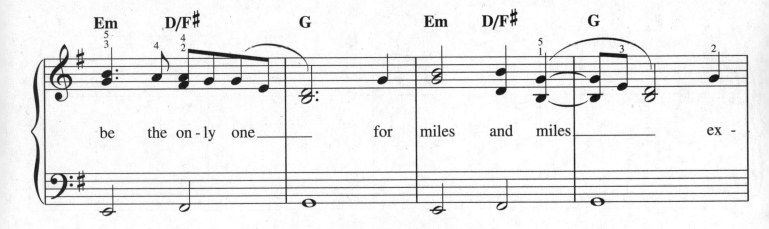

be the on - ly one_____ for miles and miles_____ ex -

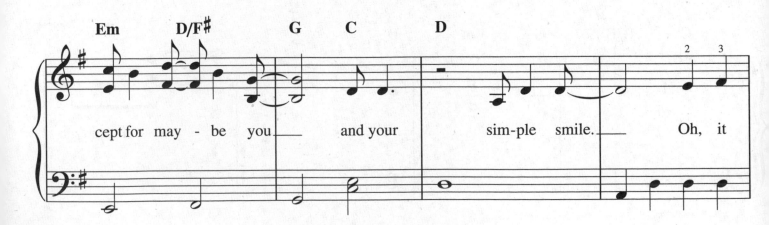

cept for may - be you__ and your sim-ple smile.__ Oh, it

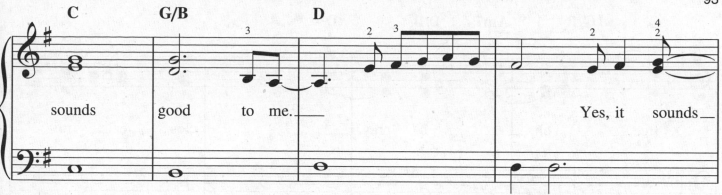

sounds   good   to me.   Yes, it   sounds

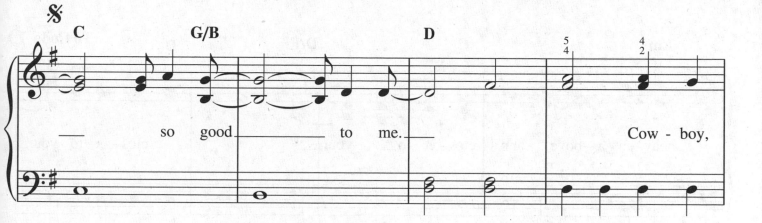

     so good   to me.   Cow - boy,

take   me   a - way.   Fly this girl as high

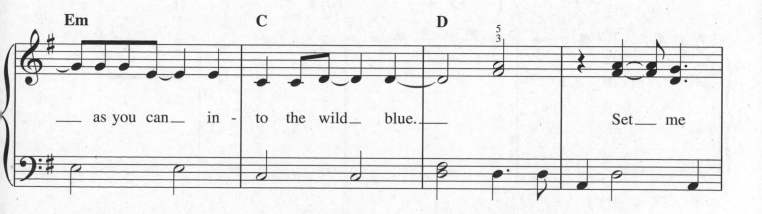

  as you can in - to the wild blue.   Set me

free,___ oh,___ I pray,___ clos - er___ to

heav - en a - bove_ and clos - er to__ you,___ clos - er to you.__

I said___ I wan-na touch the earth,___

___ I wan-na break it in___ my hands.___ I wan-na

grow some-thing wild ___ and un-rul - y ___ Oh, it sounds ___

D.S. al Coda

CODA

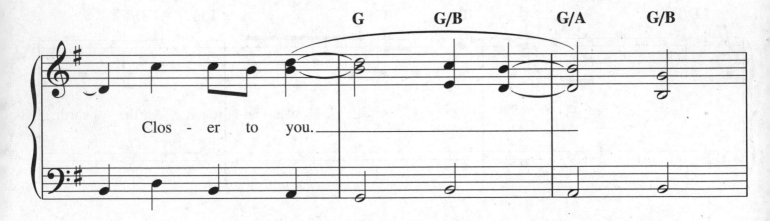

Clos - er to you. ___

Cow - boy, take me a - way, ___

clos - er to you.

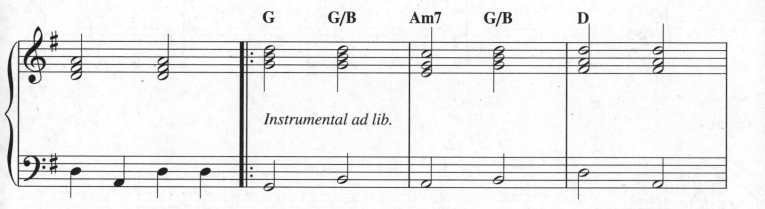

Instrumental ad lib.

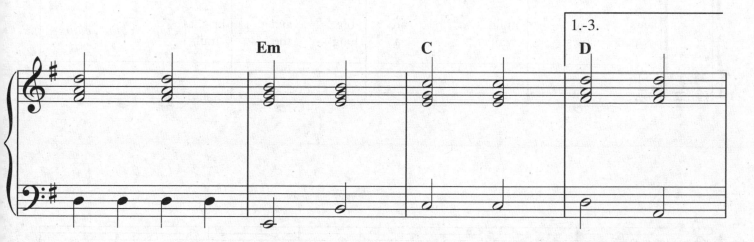

DEEP IN THE HEART OF TEXAS

Words by JUNE HERSHEY
Music by DON SWANDER

Brightly

The

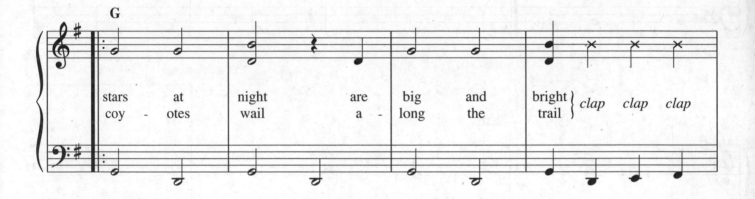

stars   at   night   are   a -   big   and   the   bright trail } *clap*   *clap*   *clap*

coy - otes   wail

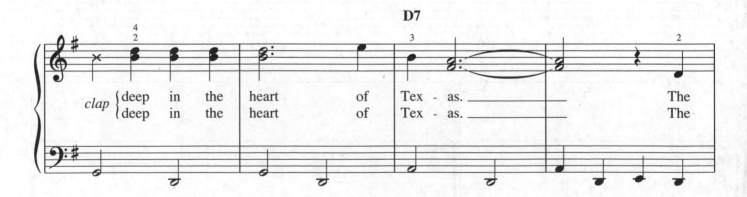

clap { deep   in   the   heart   of   Tex - as. _____   The
        deep   in   the   heart   of   Tex - as. _____   The

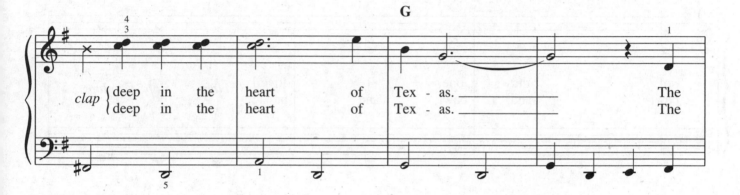

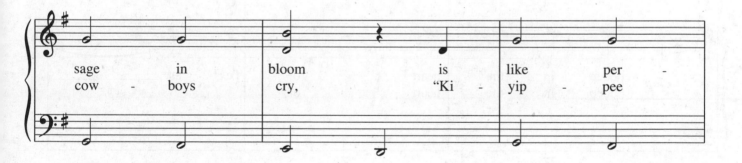

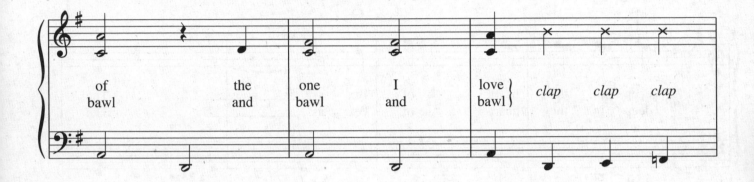

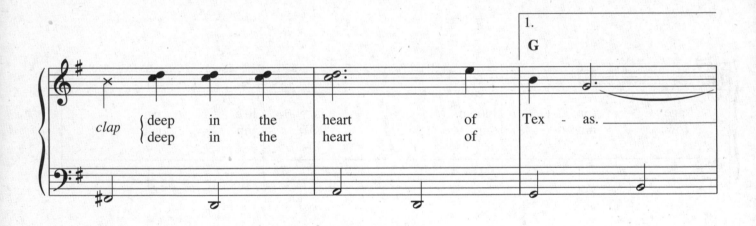

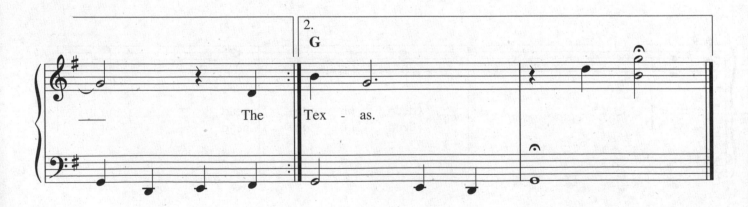

ELVIRA

Words and Music by
DALLAS FRAZIER

Moderately

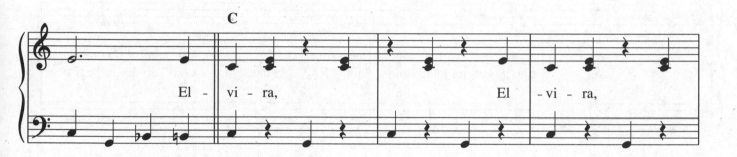

El - vi - ra,   El - vi - ra,

my heart's   on   fi - re _____ for El - vi - ra.

Eyes that look like   heav - en,   lips like cher - ry
night I'm gon - na   meet her   at the   Hun - gry House Ca -

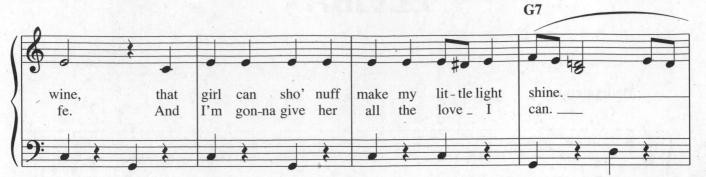

wine,   that   girl can sho' nuff   make my   lit - tle light   shine. _____
fe.   And   I'm gon-na give her   all the   love _ I   can. ___

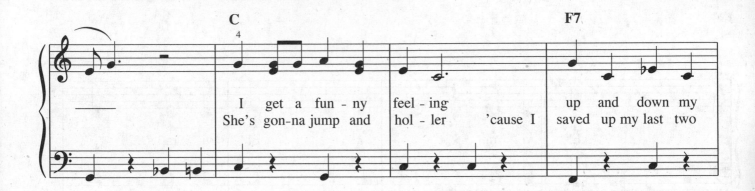

_____   I   get a fun - ny   feel - ing   up   and   down my
     She's gon-na jump and   hol - er   'cause I   saved up my last two

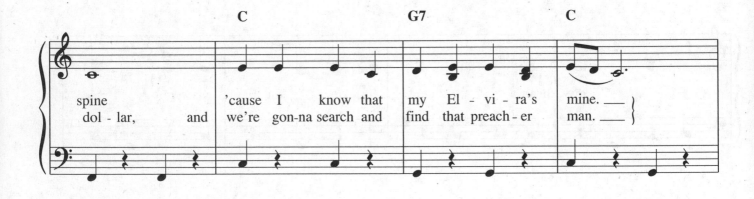

spine   'cause I   know that   my El - vi - ra's   mine. ___
dol - lar,   and   we're gon-na search and   find that preach - er   man. ___

I'm sing-in' El - vi - ra,   El - vi - ra,

my heart's on fi - re ____ for El - vi - ra.

Gid -dy -up, a oom pa - pa oom pa - pa mow mow,

gid-dy-up, a oom pa-pa oom pa-pa mow mow, hi - yo Sil - ver a -

1.
way. ____

2.
To - way. ____

FOR THE GOOD TIMES

Words and Music by
KRIS KRISTOFFERSON

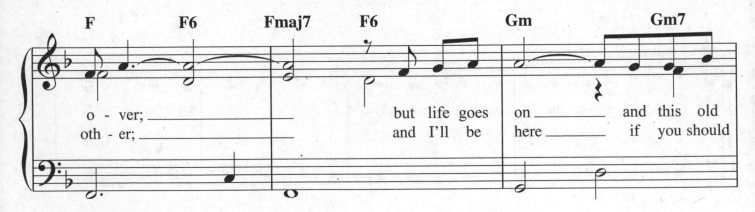

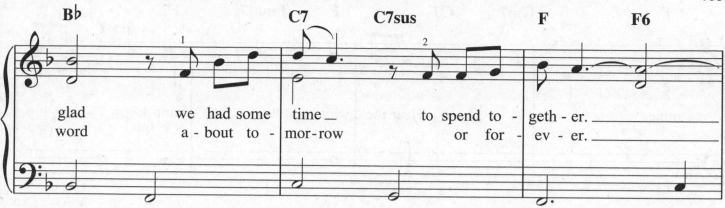

glad   we had some   time _____   to spend to - geth - er. _____
word   a - bout to - mor - row   or for - ev - er. _____

_____ There's no   need   to watch   the   bridg - es   that we're
_____ There'll be   time   e - nough   for   sad - ness   when you

burn - ing. _____ Lay your   head _____ up - on my
leave me. _____

pil - low, _____ hold your warm   and ten - der   bod - y   close to

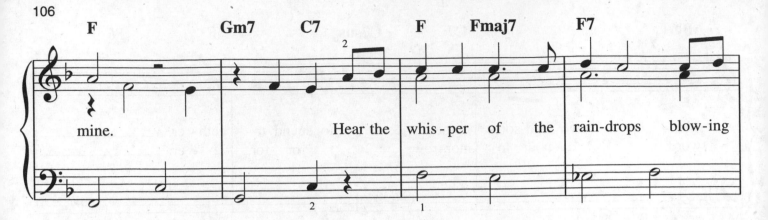

mine. | Hear the whis-per of the rain-drops blow-ing

soft a-gainst the win-dow and make be-lieve you

love me one more time, _____ for the

good times. _____ | I'll get a- good times. _____

GAMES PEOPLE PLAY

Words and Music by
JOE SOUND

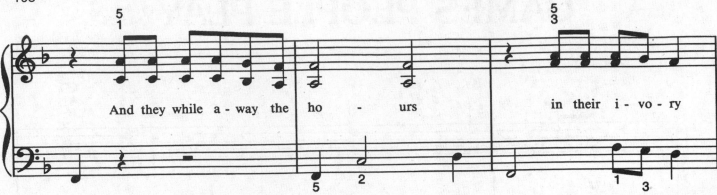

And they while a - way the ho - urs in their i - vo - ry

C

tow - ers, 'Til they're cov - ered up with flow - ers, In the

C   F   **Chorus**

back of a black lim - ou - sine. La, da, da, da,

da, da, da. La, da, da, da, da, da, dee.

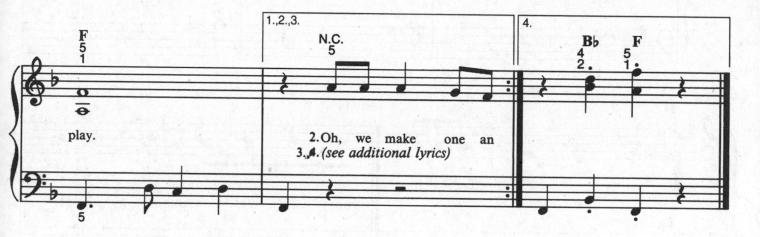

Additional Lyrics

2. Oh, we make one another cry,
   Break a heart, then we say goodbye,
   Cross our hearts and we hope to die,
   That the other was to blame.
   Neither one will ever give in,
   So we gaze at an eight by ten,
   Thinkin' 'bout the things that might have been,
   It's a dirty rotten shame.

   Chorus

3. People walkin up to you
   Singin' "Glory Hallelujah!"
   And they're tryin' to sock it to ya
   In the name of the Lord.
   They gonna teach you how to meditate,
   Read your horoscope and cheat your fate,
   And furthermore to hell with hate.
   Come on get on board.

   Chorus

4. Look around, tell me what you see.
   What's happenin' to you and me?
   God grant me the serenity
   To remember who I am.
   'Cause you're givin' up your sanity
   For your pride and your vanity.
   Turn your back on humanity,
   And don't give a da da da da da.

   Chorus

FRIENDS IN LOW PLACES

Words and Music by DEWAYNE BLACKWELL
and EARL BUD LEE

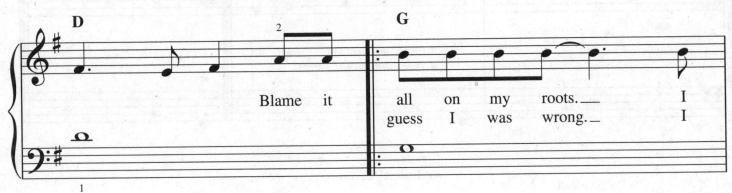

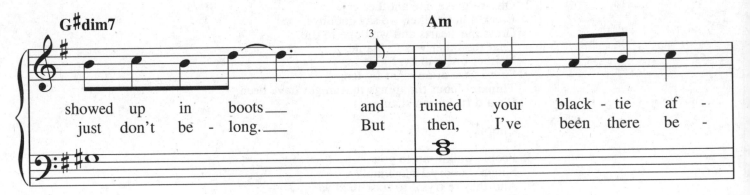

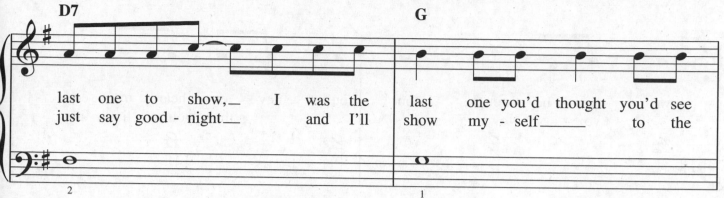

last one to show,— I was the last one you'd thought you'd see
just say good - night— and I'll show my - self——— to the

there.——— And I saw the sur - prise— and the
door.——— Hey, I did - n't mean— to

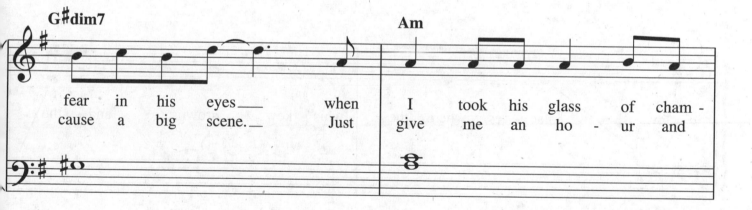

fear in his eyes— when I took his glass of cham -
cause a big scene.— Just give me an ho - ur and

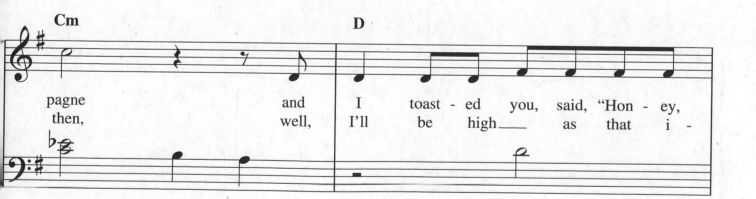

pagne and I toast - ed you, said, "Hon - ey,
then, well, I'll be high— as that i -

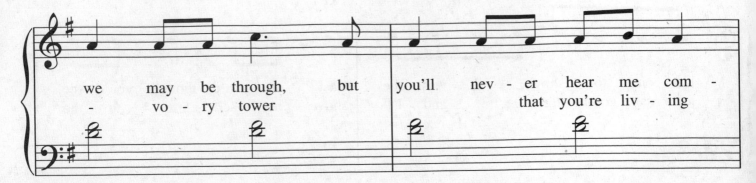

we may be through, but you'll nev - er hear me com -
- vo - ry tower that you're liv - ing

plain."
in.
'Cause I've got friends in

low plac - es, where the whis - key drowns and the

beer chas - es my blues a - way and I'll

be o - kay. Yeah, I'm not big____ on

so - cial grac - es. Think I'll slip on____ down to the

O - a - sis. Oh,____ I've got friends in low____

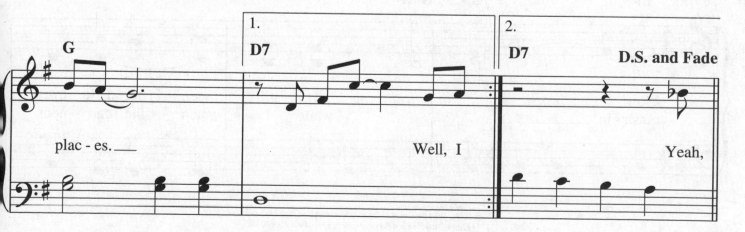

plac - es. ____ Well, I Yeah,

GALVESTON

Words and Music by
JIM WEBB

Moderate Rock

Gal - ves - ton,___ oh, Gal - ves -
Gal - ves - ton,___ oh, Gal - ves -

ton, I still hear your sea - winds
ton, I still hear your sea - waves

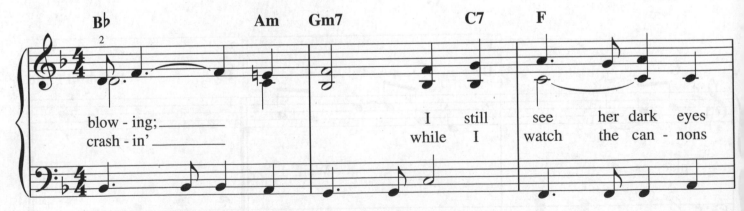

blow - ing;___ I still see her dark eyes
crash - in'___ while I watch the can - nons

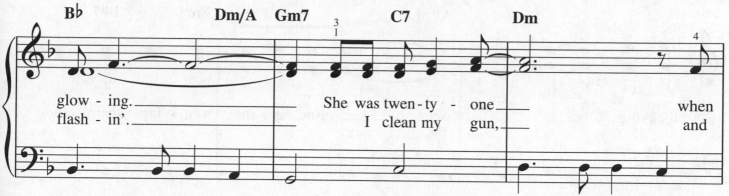

glow - ing._____ She was twen-ty - one_____ when

flash - in'._____ I clean my gun,_____ and

I left Gal - ves - ton._____

dream of Gal - ves - ton._____

1.

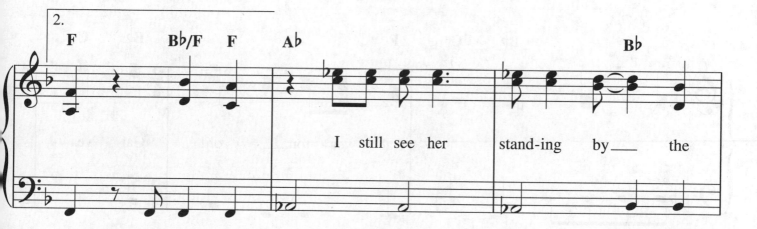

2.

I still see her stand-ing by____ the

wa - ter,

stand-ing there

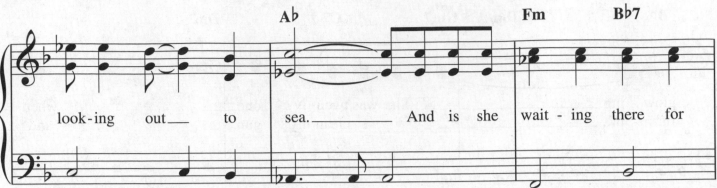

looking out to sea. And is she waiting there for

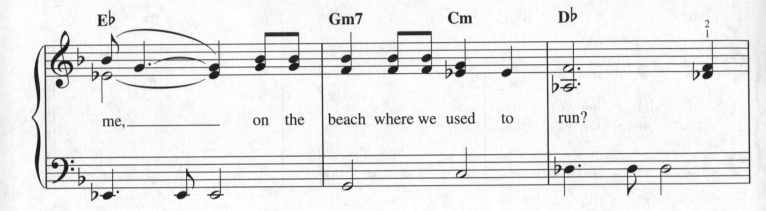

me, on the beach where we used to run?

Galveston, oh! Galves-

ton, I am so afraid of

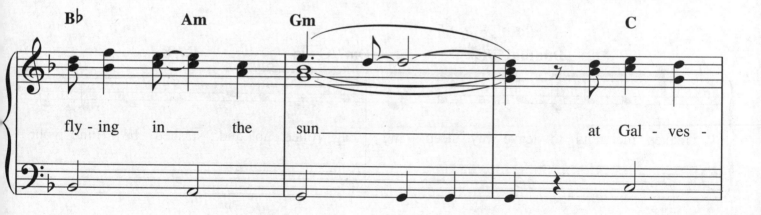

GENTLE ON MY MIND

Words and Music by
JOHN HARTFORD

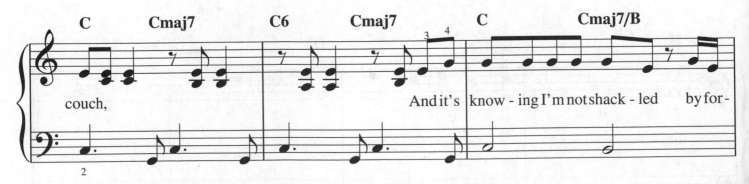

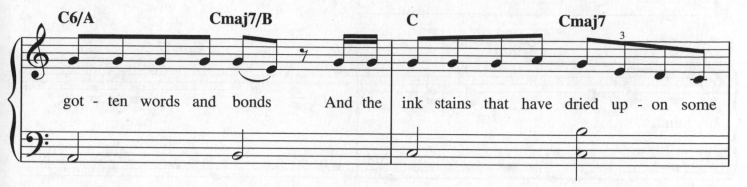

got - ten words and bonds And the ink stains that have dried up - on some

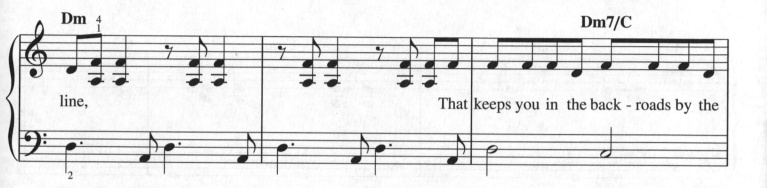

line, That keeps you in the back - roads by the

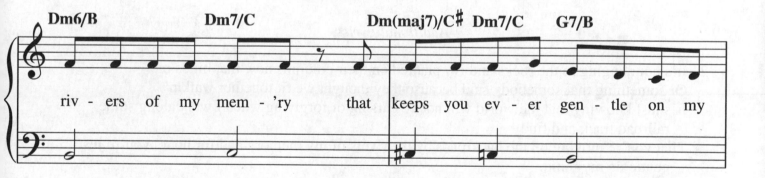

riv - ers of my mem - 'ry that keeps you ev - er gen - tle on my

mind. 2. It's not

Additional Lyrics

2. It's not clinging to the rocks and ivy planted on their columns now that binds me
   Or something that somebody said because they thought we fit together walkin'.
   It's just knowing that the world will not be cursing or forgiving when I walk along some
   railroad track and find
   That you're moving on the backroads by the rivers of my memory and for hours you're just
   gentle on my mind.

3. Though the wheat fields and the clotheslines and junkyards and the highways come between us
   And some other woman crying to her mother 'cause she turned away and I was gone.
   I still run in silence, tears of joy might stain my face and summer sun might burn me 'til I'm blind.
   But not to where I cannot see you walkin' on the backroads by the rivers flowing gentle on my mind.

4. I dip my cup of soup back from the gurglin' cracklin' caldron in some train yard
   My beard, a rough'ning coal pile and a dirty hat pulled low across my face.
   Through cupped hands 'round a tin can I pretend I hold you to my breast and find
   That you're waving from the backroads by the rivers of my memory ever smilin' ever
   gentle on my mind.

THE GREATEST MAN I NEVER KNEW

Words and Music by RICHARD LEIGH
and LAYNG MARTINE, JR.

1. The great-est man I _____ nev-er knew _____
2. The great-est man I _____ nev-er knew _____
3. (See additional lyrics)

lived just down the hall, _____ and ev-'ry day we said hel - lo _____
came home late ev - 'ry night, _____ he nev-er had too much to say, _____

but nev - er touched at all. ____
too much was on his mind. ____
He was in his
I nev - er real - ly

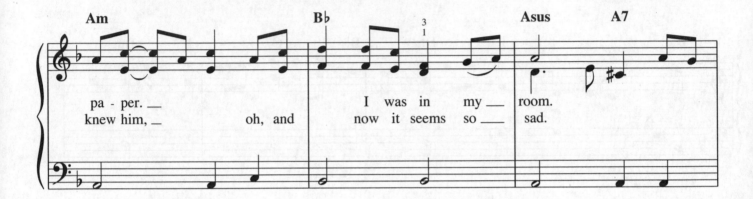

pa - per. ____
knew him, ____ oh, and
I was in my ____ room.
now it seems so ____ sad.

To Coda ⊕

How was I to know ____ he thought ____ I
Ev - 'ry - thing he gave ____ to us ____ took
hung the ____ moon?
all he ____ had.

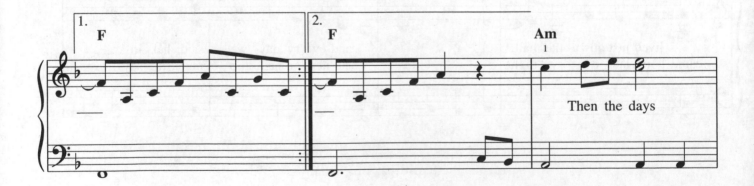

Then the days

turned in - to years, ___ and the mem - 'ries to black ___ and white. ___

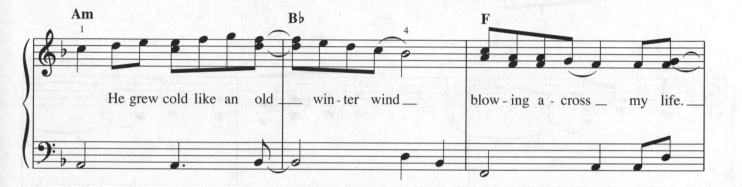

He grew cold like an old ___ win - ter wind ___ blow - ing a - cross ___ my life. ___

D.S. al Coda   **CODA**

thought   I ___ knew. ___
rit.

Additional Lyrics

3. The greatest words I never heard
   I guess I'll never hear.
   The man I thought could never die
      has been dead almost a year.
   Oh, he was good at bus'ness,
      but there was bus'ness left to do.
   He never said he loved me.
   Guess he thought I knew.

GRANDPA
(Tell Me 'Bout the Good Old Days)

Words and Music by
JAMIE O'HARA

Grand - pa, __ ... tell me 'bout the good old days. __
Grand - pa, __ ... ev - 'ry - thing is chang - in' fast. __

Some-times ___ it feels like this world's gone cra-
We call ___ it pro - gress, but I just don't know.

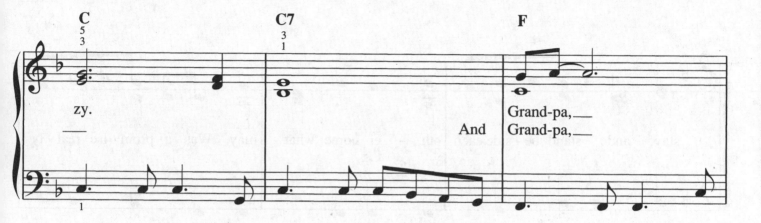

C **C7** **F**

zy.

And Grand-pa, ___
Grand-pa, ___

B♭

take me back to yes - ter - day ___ when the line ___ be-tween
let's wan-der back in - to the past. ___ Then paint me ___ the

F **C7**

right and wrong did - n't seem ___ so
pic - ture ___ of ___ long ___ a -

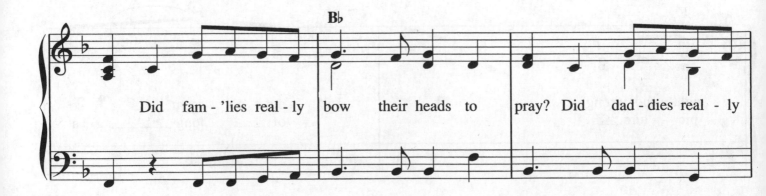

nev - er go a - way? Oh, _____ oh, _____ Grand - pa, _____

tell me 'bout the good old _ days. _

days. _____

Oh, _____ oh, _____ Grand - pa, _____

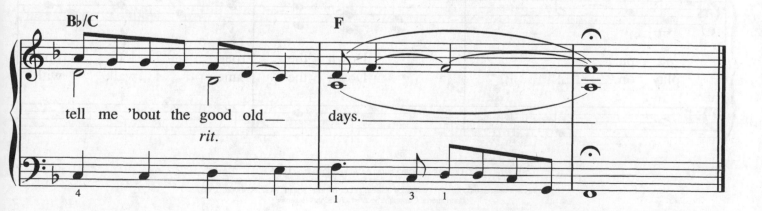

tell me 'bout the good old _ days. _____

rit.

GREEN GREEN GRASS OF HOME

Words and Music by
CURLY PUTMAN

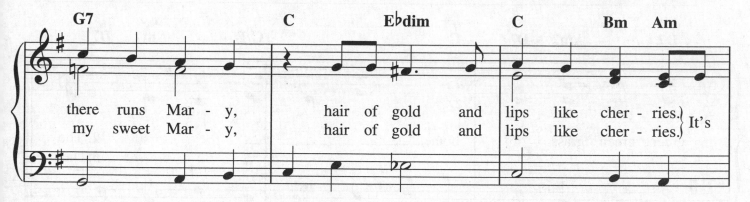

there runs Mar - y,   hair of gold and   lips like cher - ries.
my sweet Mar - y,   hair of gold and   lips like cher - ries. It's

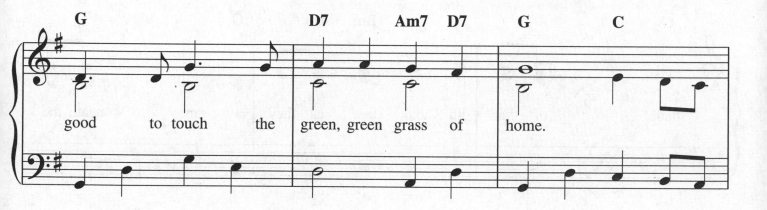

good   to touch the   green, green grass of   home.

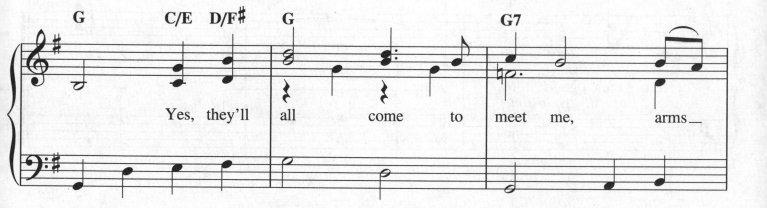

Yes, they'll all   come to meet me,   arms___

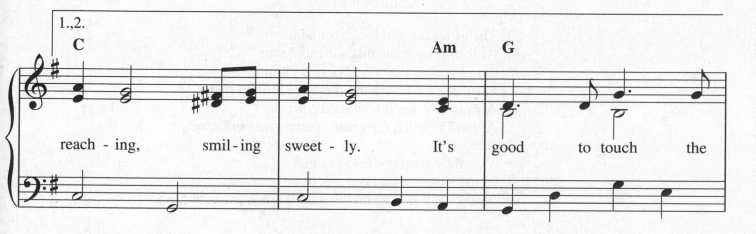

reach - ing,   smil - ing sweet - ly.   It's   good   to touch the

green, green grass of home._____ 2. The
3. Then

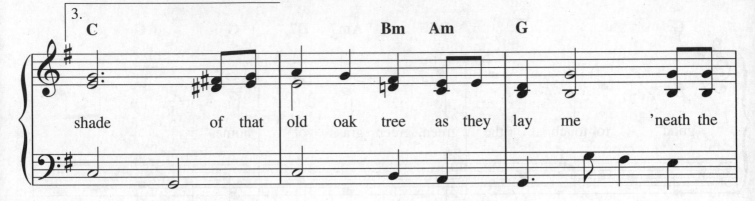

shade of that old oak tree as they lay me 'neath the

green, green grass of home._____
rit. e dim.

Additional Lyrics

3. Then I awake and look around me
At four gray walls that surround me,
And I realize that I was only dreaming.
For there's a guard and there's a sad old padre,
Arm in arm we'll walk at daybreak,
Again I'll touch the green, green grass of home.

Yes, they'll all come to see me
In the shade of that old oak tree
As they lay me 'neath the green, green grass of home.

HARD ROCK BOTTOM OF YOUR HEART

Words and Music by
HUGH PRESTWOOD

Country two-beat (♩ = 80)

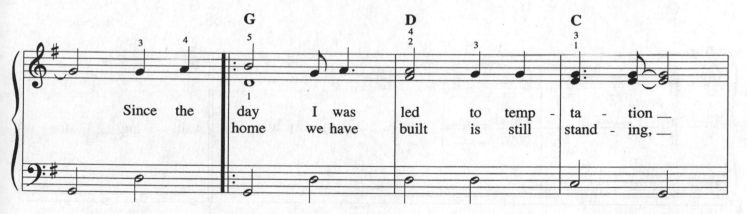

Since the day I was led to temp - ta - tion ___
home we have built is still stand - ing, ___

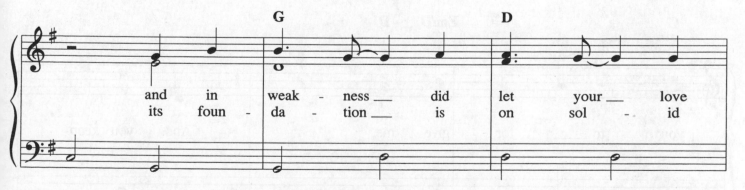

and in weak - ness ___ did let your ___ love
its foun - da - tion ___ is on sol - id

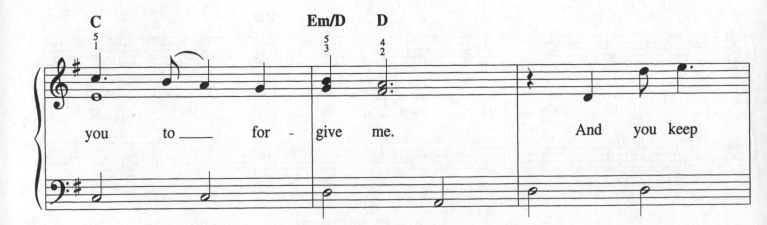

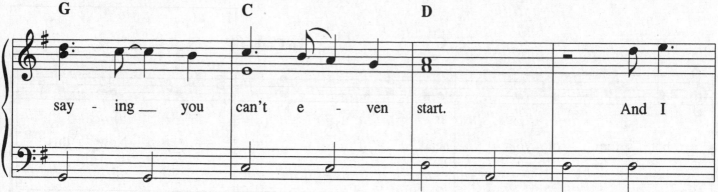

say - ing __ you can't e - ven start. And I

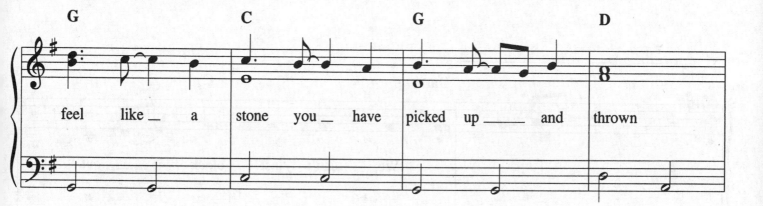

feel like __ a stone you __ have picked up __ and thrown

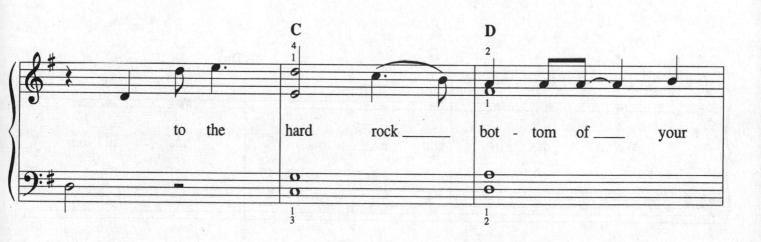

to the hard rock _____ bot - tom of ___ your

heart, to the hard rock _____

D   **G**   **To Coda**   **1.**

bot - tom of your heart.   Now this

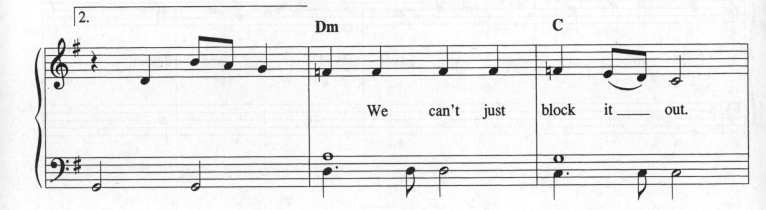

2.   **Dm**   **C**

We can't just block it ___ out.

Dm   **C**   **Dm**

We've got to talk it ___ out   un - til our

C   **G**   **Dm7**

hearts get back _ in ___ touch.   I need your

love, I miss it. I can't go on like this __ it

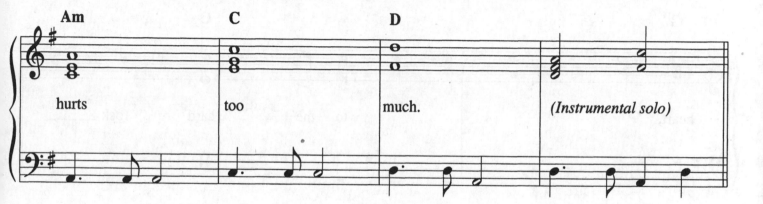

hurts too much. *(Instrumental solo)*

D.S. al Coda

And I keep

CODA

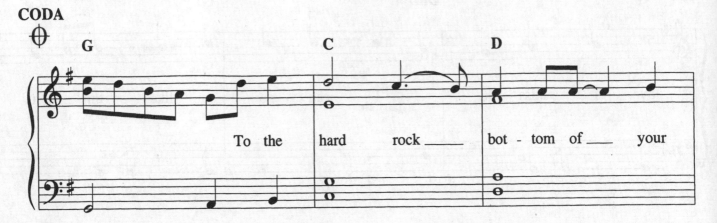

To the hard rock _____ bot - tom of _____ your

heart, to the hard rock _____

bot - tom _____ of your heart.

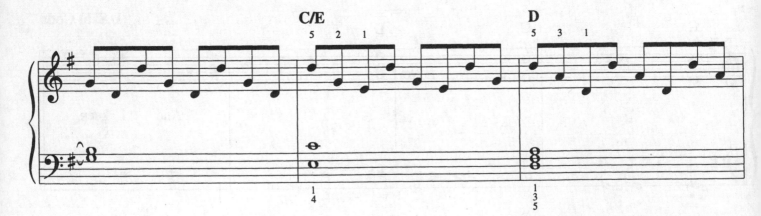

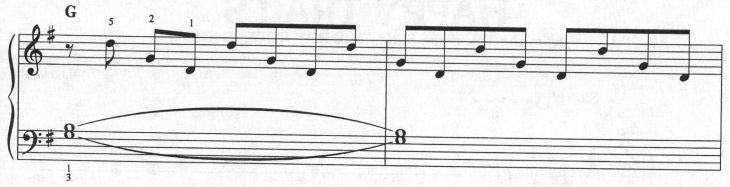

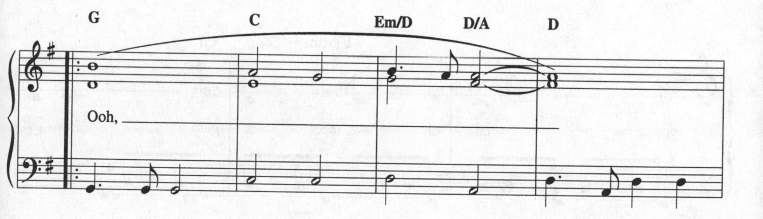

Ooh,

ooh.

HAPPY TRAILS
from the Television Series THE ROY ROGERS SHOW

Words and Music by
DALE EVANS

then. Who cares a - bout the clouds when we're to -

geth - er? Just sing a song and bring the sun - ny

weath - er. Hap-py trails to you till we

meet a - gain. | gain.
1. F | 2. F Bb F6
Hap-py
rit.

HE STOPPED LOVING HER TODAY

Words and Music by BOBBY BRADDOCK
and CURLY PUTMAN

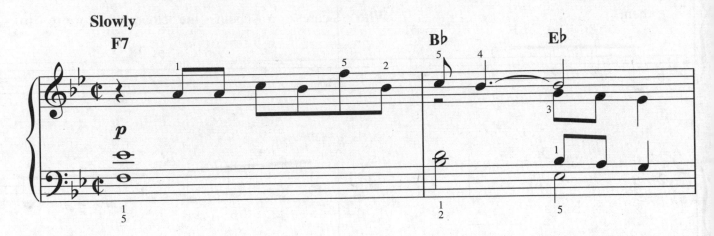

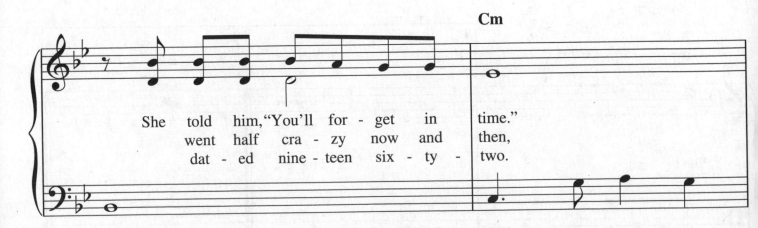

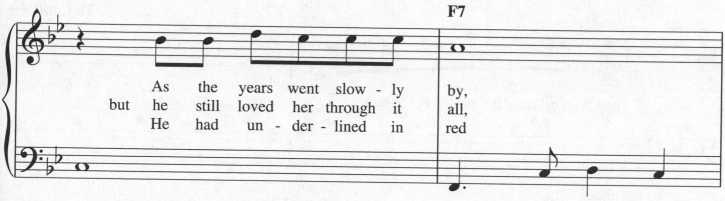

F7

As the years went slow - ly by,
but he still loved her through it all,
He had un - der - lined in red

B♭

she still preyed up - on his mind.
hop - ing she'd come back a - gain.
ev - 'ry sin - gle "I love you."

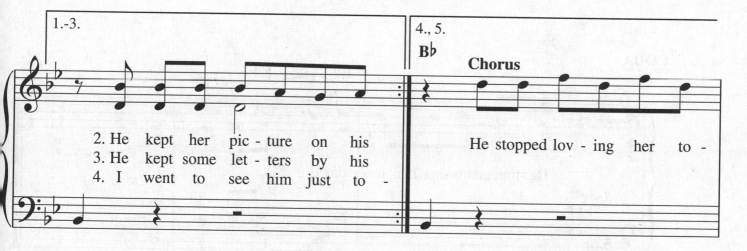

1.-3.

2. He kept her pic - ture on his
3. He kept some let - ters by his
4. I went to see him just to -

4., 5.

B♭

Chorus

He stopped lov - ing her to -

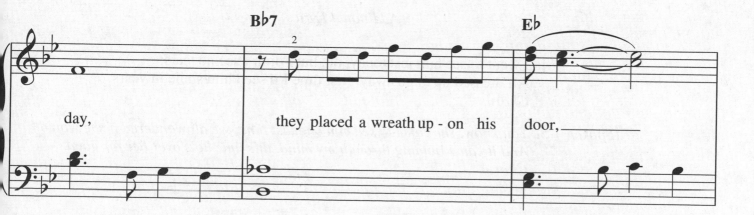

B♭7

day,

they placed a wreath up - on his

E♭

door,_____

and soon they'll car - ry him a - way.

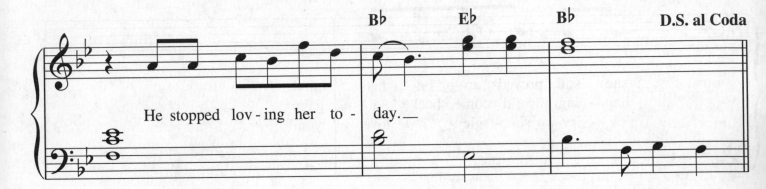

He stopped lov - ing her to - day.

He stopped lov - ing her to - day.

Additional Lyrics

4. I went to see him just today, oh, but I didn't see no tears;
   All dressed up to go away, first time I'd seen him smile in years.
   Chorus

(Spoken:) 5. *You know, she came to see him one last time; we all wondered if she would.*
   And it came running through my mind, this time he's over her for good.
   Chorus

HELLO DARLIN'

Words and Music by
CONWAY TWITTY

Moderate Country Waltz

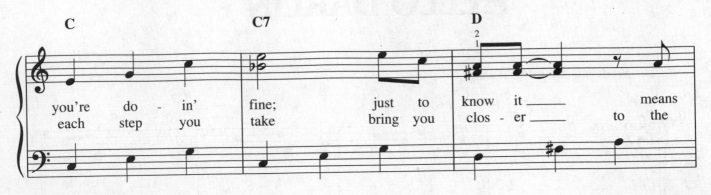

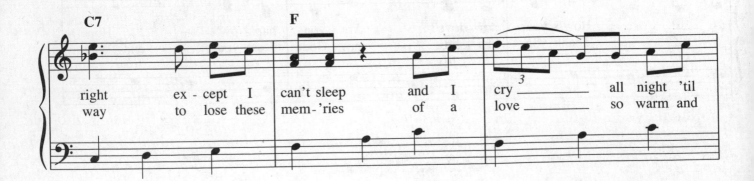

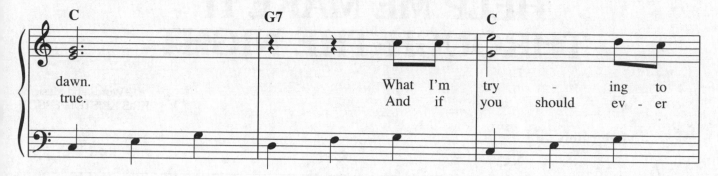

dawn.
true.

What I'm try - ing to
And if you should ev - er

say it is, "I love you ___ and I ___ miss you, ___ and
find it in your heart to ___ for - give _ me, ___

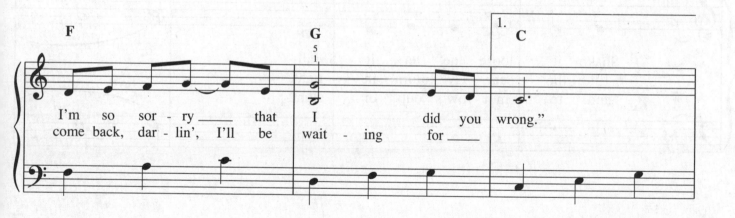

I'm so sor - ry ___ that I did you wrong."
come back, dar - lin', I'll be wait - ing for ___

Look up you.

HELP ME MAKE IT THROUGH THE NIGHT

Words and Music by
KRIS KRISTOFFERSON

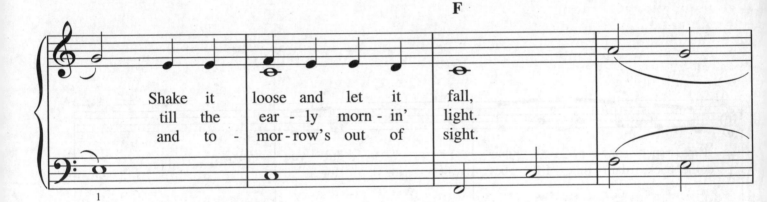

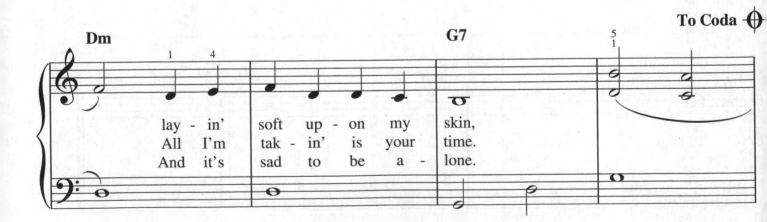

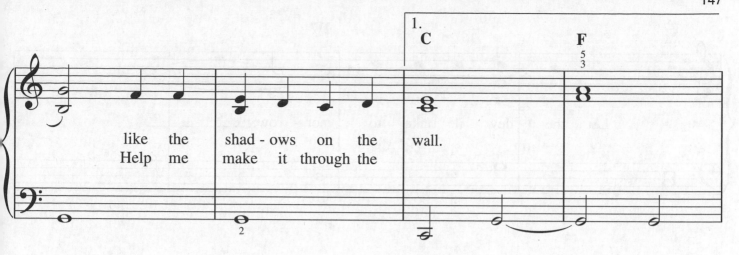

like the   shad - ows   on   the   wall.
Help me   make   it through the

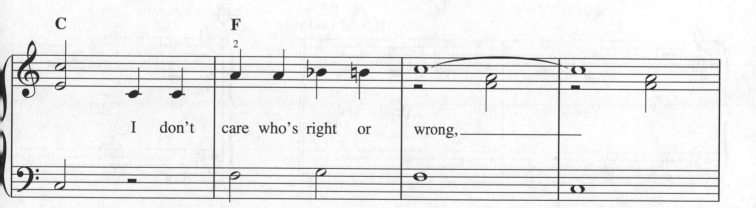

Come and   lay down by my   night.

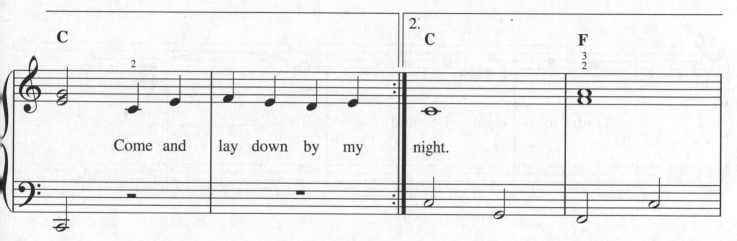

I   don't   care who's right or   wrong,_____

I   don't   try   to   un - der - stand._____

Let the dev - il take to - mor - row; _____

D **G7**

Lord, to - night I need a friend. _____

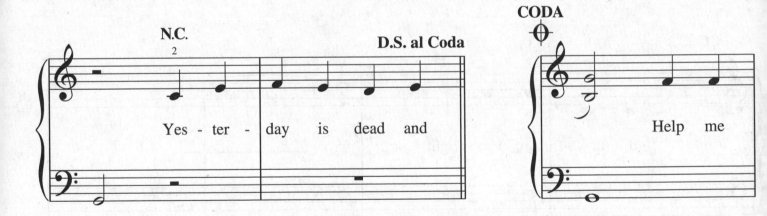

N.C. **D.S. al Coda** **CODA**

Yes - ter - day is dead and Help me

C **F** **C**

make it through the night.

HEY, GOOD LOOKIN'

Words and Music by
HANK WILLIAMS

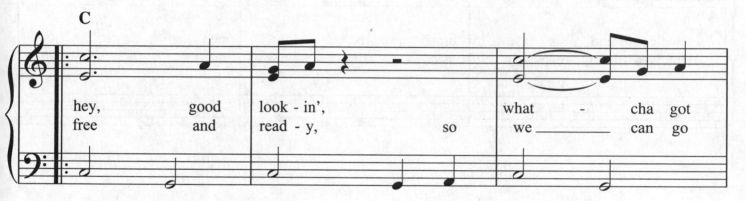

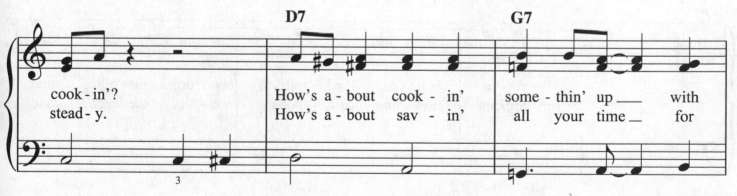

150

ba - by,   don't ____ you think   may - be,
look - in',   I   know ____ I've been   took - en.

D7   **G7**   **C**

we could find us a   brand new rec - i - pe?
How's a - bout keep - in' stead - y com - pa - ny?

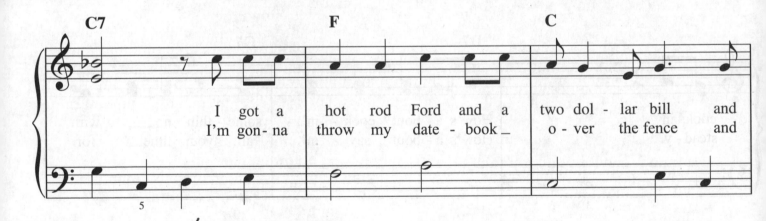

C7   **F**   **C**

I got a   hot rod Ford and a   two dol - lar bill   and
I'm gon - na   throw my date - book __ o - ver the fence   and

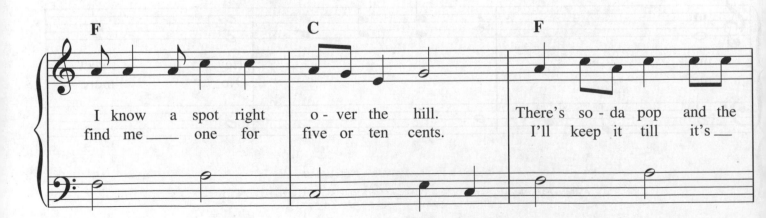

F   **C**   **F**

I know a spot right   o - ver the hill.   There's so - da pop and the
find me __ one for   five or ten cents.   I'll keep it till it's __

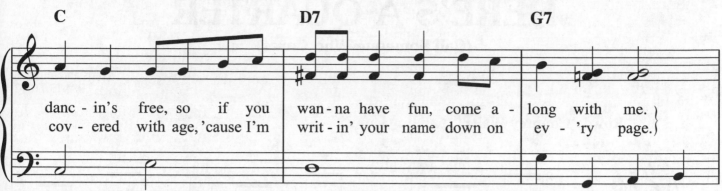

C   **D7**   **G7**

danc - in's   free,   so   if   you   wan - na   have   fun,   come a -   long   with   me.

cov - ered   with   age, 'cause I'm   writ - in'   your   name   down on   ev - 'ry   page.

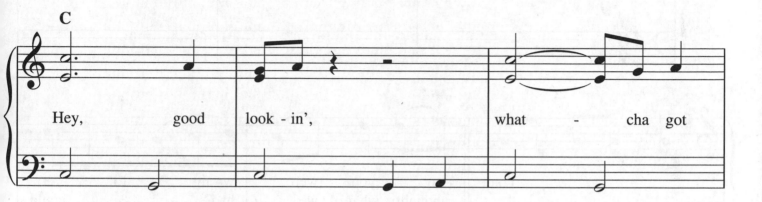

C

Hey,   good   look - in',   what - cha   got

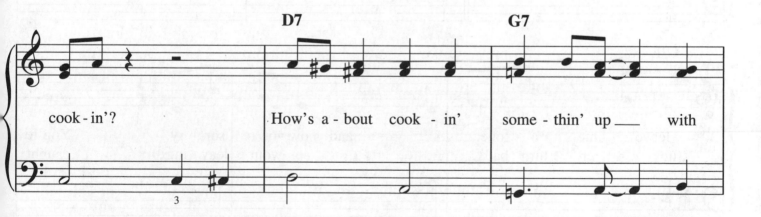

                     D7   **G7**

cook - in'?   How's a - bout cook - in'   some - thin' up ___ with

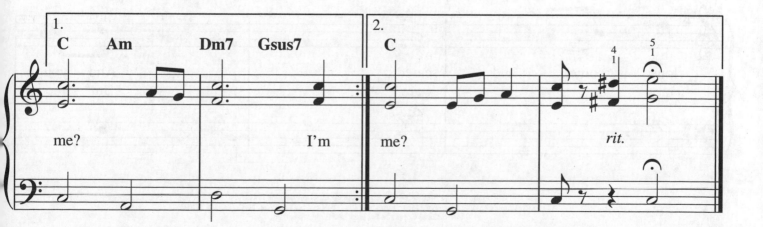

1.

C   **Am**   **Dm7**   **Gsus7**   **2.**   **C**

me?   I'm   me?   *rit.*

HERE'S A QUARTER
(Call Someone Who Cares)

Words and Music by
TRAVIS TRITT

say   you'd   be___   hap - py   if   you could   just___ come   back
fact   is   you've   run.___   Girl,___ that   can't___ be   un -

home.___   Well, here's a   quar - ter.   Call___   some - one   who
done.___   So   here's a   quar - ter.   Call___   some - one   who

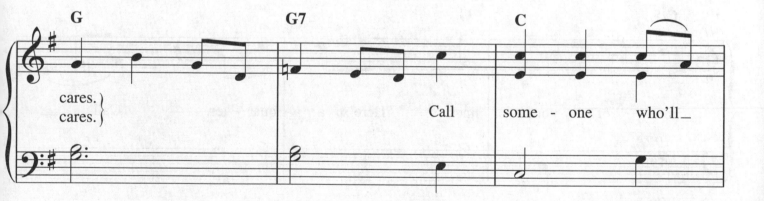

cares.}
cares.}   Call   some - one   who'll___

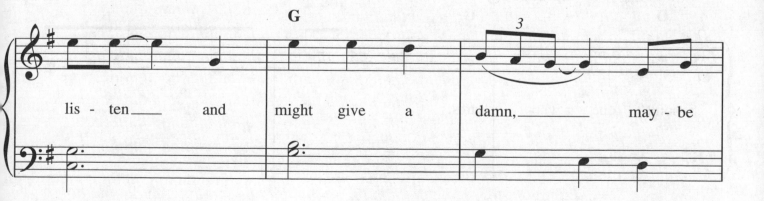

lis - ten___   and   might give a   damn,_____   may - be

one of____ your sor - did____ af - fairs.____

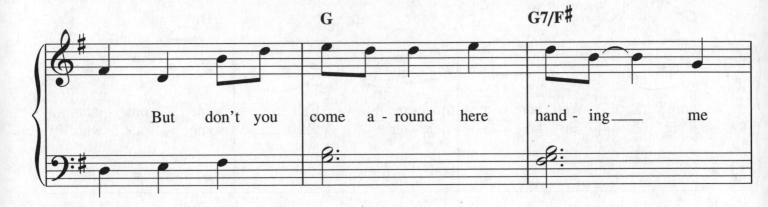

But don't you come a - round here hand - ing____ me

none of your lines. Here's a quar - ter. Call____

To Coda ⊕

some - one who cares.

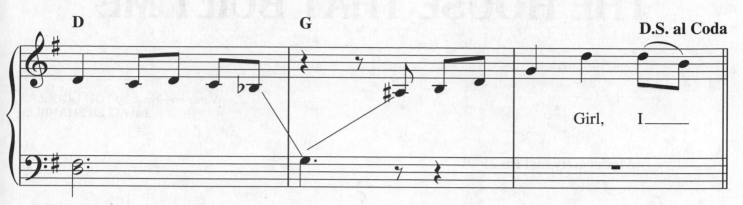

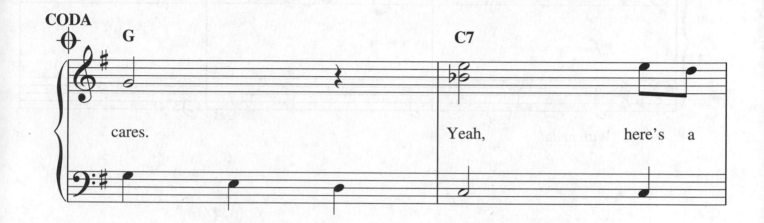

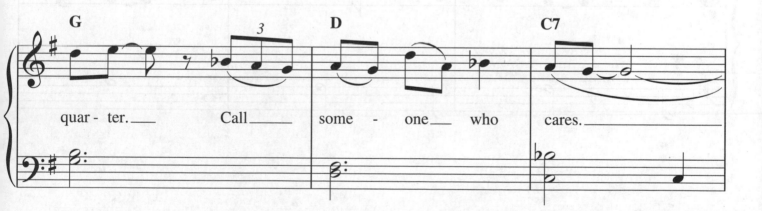

THE HOUSE THAT BUILT ME

Words and Music by TOM DOUGLAS
and ALLEN SHAMBLIN

Moderately fast (in 2)

With pedal

I know they say ___ you

can't go home a - gain. ___

I just had to come ___ back one last time.

Ma'am, I know_ you don't know_ me from

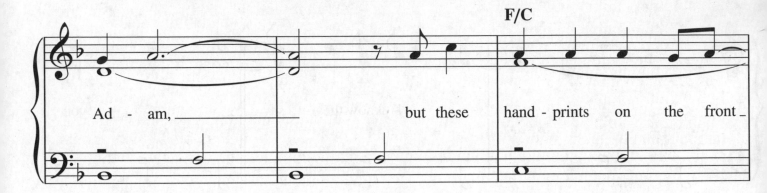

Ad - am,_____ but these hand - prints on the front_

___ steps are mine._____ Up those stairs_

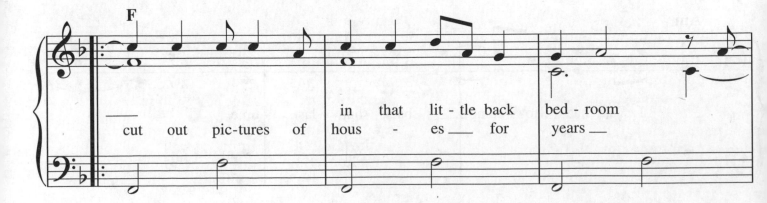

___ cut out pic-tures of hous - es ___ for years___ in that lit-tle back bed - room

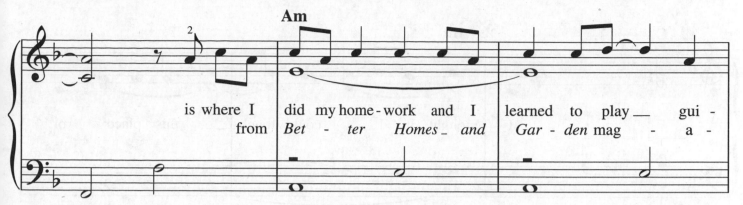

Am

is where I did my home-work and I learned to play_ gui-
from *Bet - ter Homes_ and Gar - den* mag - a -

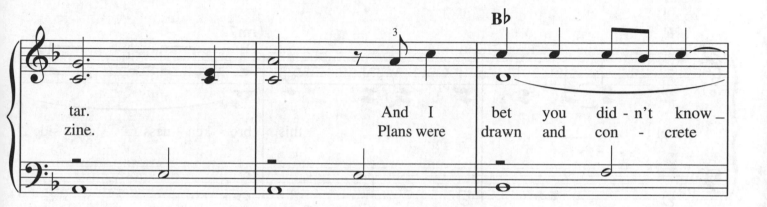

Bb

tar. And I bet you did - n't know_
zine. Plans were drawn and con - crete

___ poured; and nail_ by nail and that_ live oak my
poured; and nail_ by nail and board_ by board,

F/C   **Csus**

fav - 'rite dog_ is bur - ied in _____ the yard. _____
Dad-dy gave life to Ma - ma's dream. ____

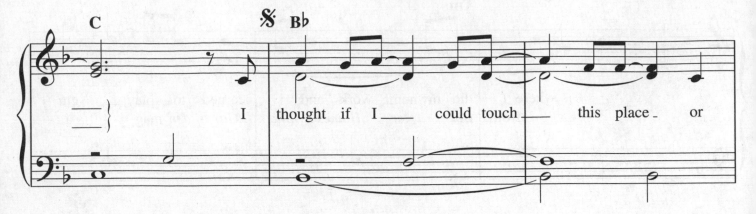

find my - self. If

((1.,2.) I could just __ come in, I swear I'll leave.)
((D.S.) I could walk __ a - round, I swear I'll leave.)

To Coda ⊕

Won't take noth - in' but a mem - o - ry _____ from the

house that _____ built __ me.

162

1.

Ma - ma

2.

Dm

You leave home, _ you move on _ and you

F

do the best _ you can.

Gm7

I got lost _ in

this old world _ and for - got

Bb

who I

I CAN LOVE YOU LIKE THAT

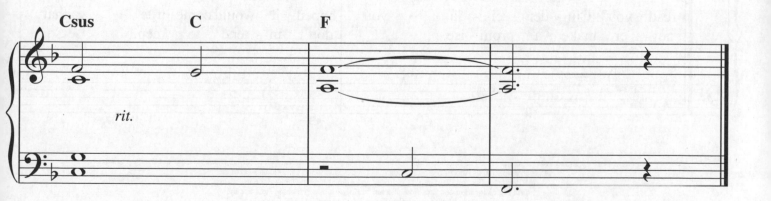

I CAN LOVE YOU LIKE THAT

Words and Music by MARIBETH DERRY,
JENNIFER KIMBALL and STEVE DIAMOND

They

read you Cin- der- el- la   you   hoped it would come true   that
nev- er make a prom- ise   I   don't in- tend to keep.   So,

F

one day your Prince Charm-ing would come ___ res - cue you. ___ You
when I say for - ev - er, for - ev - er's what I mean.

G7sus

C

like ro - man - tic mov - ies; you
I'm no Ca - sa - no - va, but

Em

nev - er will for - get the
I swear this much is true:

F

way you felt when Ro - me - o kissed
I'll be hold - ing noth - ing back when

G7sus

Ju - li - et. ___
it comes to you. You

Em7

All this time that you've been
dream of love that's ev - er

F

wait - ing,
last - ing. Well,

Em7 / **F**

you don't have to wait no _____ more.
ba - by, o - pen up your _____ eyes.

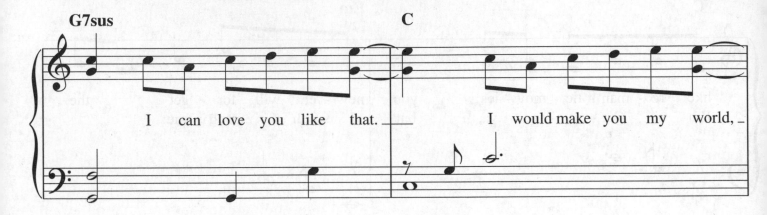

G7sus / **C**

I can love you like that. ___ I would make you my world, ___

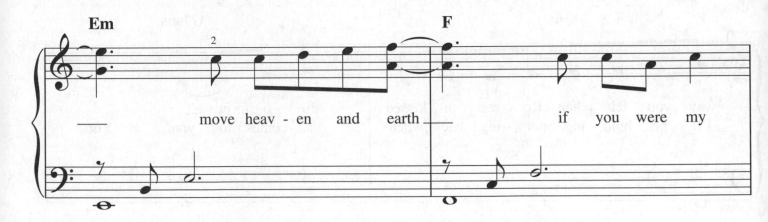

Em / **F**

___ move heav - en and earth ___ if you were my

G7sus / **C**

girl. I will give you my heart, ___ be all that you need,

Em   F

show you you're ev - 'ry - thing that's pre - cious to

Bb

me.   If you give me a chance,

G7sus   1. C

I can love you like that.

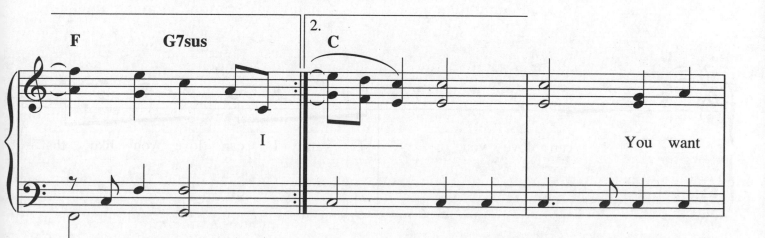

F   G7sus   2. C

I   You want

ten-der-ness, I got ten - der-ness. And I see through to the

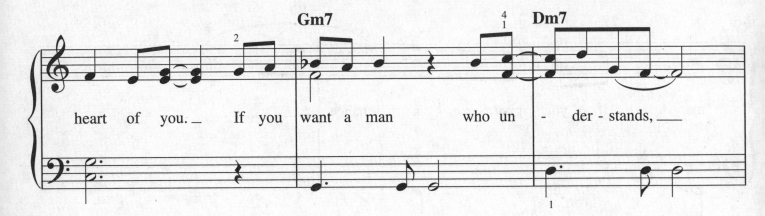

heart of you. _ If you want a man who un - der - stands, ___

you don't have to look ver - y far. ___

___ I can love you, I can, I can love you like that. _

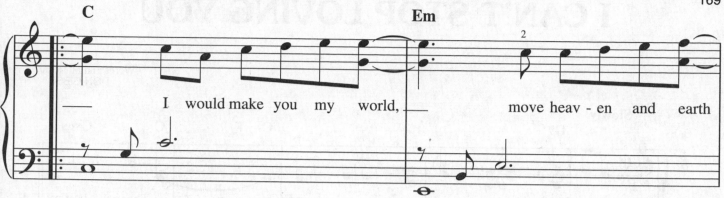

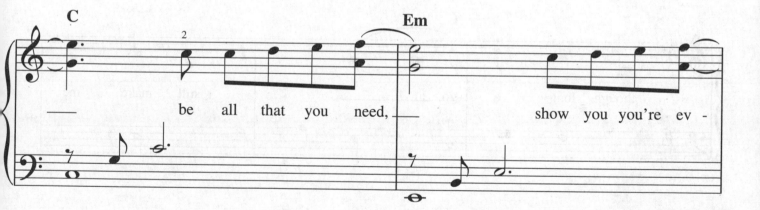

I CAN'T STOP LOVING YOU

Words and Music by
DON GIBSON

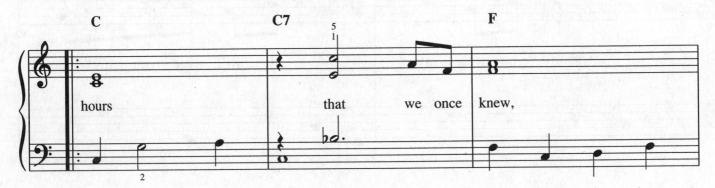

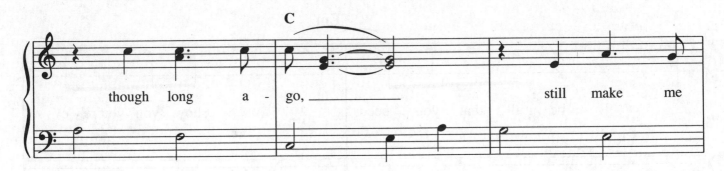

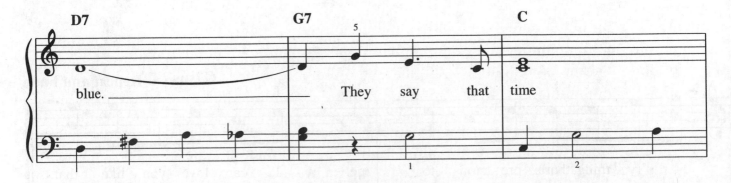

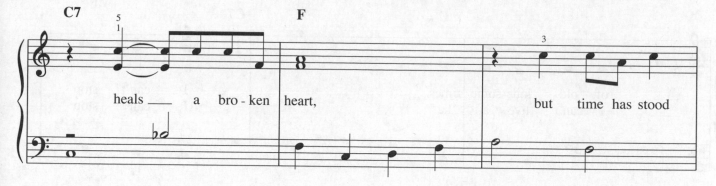

heals ___ a bro-ken heart, but time has stood

still _____ since we've been a - part.

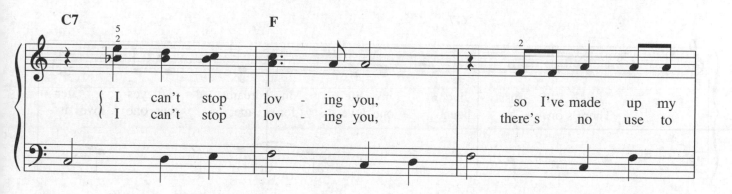

I can't stop lov - ing you, so I've made up my
I can't stop lov - ing you, there's no use to

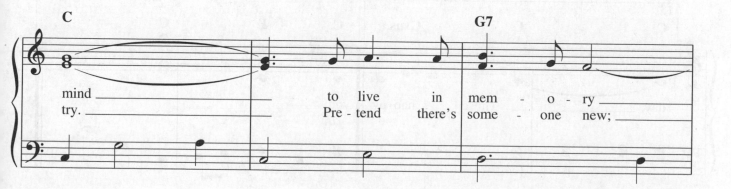

mind _____ to live in mem - o - ry ___
try. _____ Pre - tend there's some - one new; ___

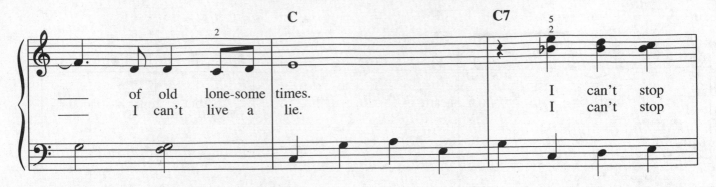

C   **C7**

_____ of old lone-some times.
_____ I can't live a lie.   I can't stop
                              I can't stop

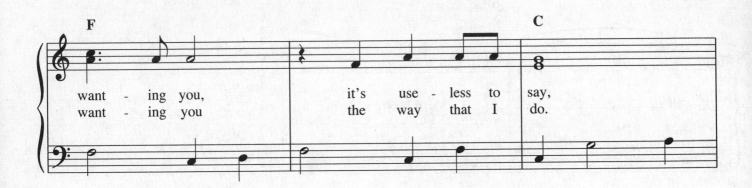

F   **C**

want - ing you,   it's use - less to say,
want - ing you   the way that I do.

G7

so I'll just   live   my life   in dreams   of yes - ter -
There's on - ly   been   one love   for me,   that one love is

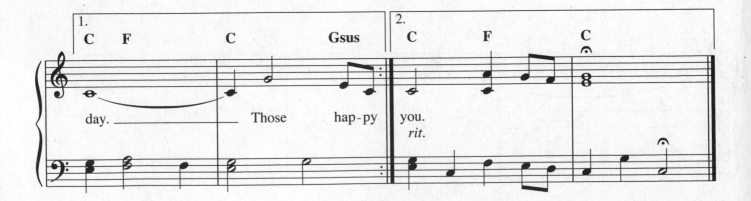

1.
C   F   C   Gsus

day. _____ Those hap-py

2.
C   F   C

you.
rit.

I FALL TO PIECES

Words and Music by HANK COCHRAN
and HARLAN HOWARD

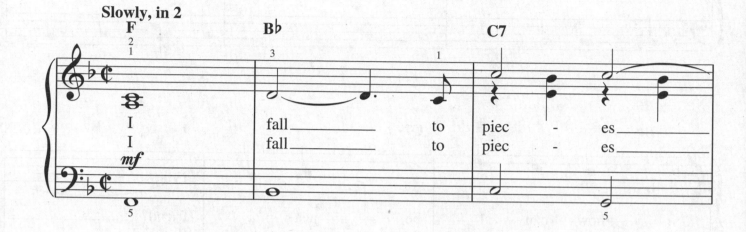

fall _____ to piec - es _____
fall _____ to piec - es _____

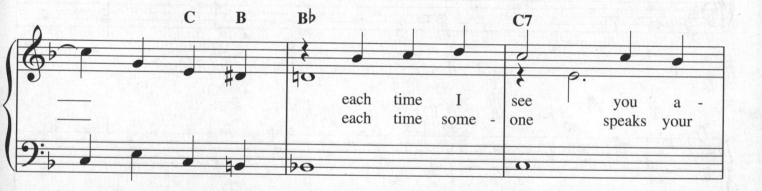

each time I see you a -
each time some - one speaks your

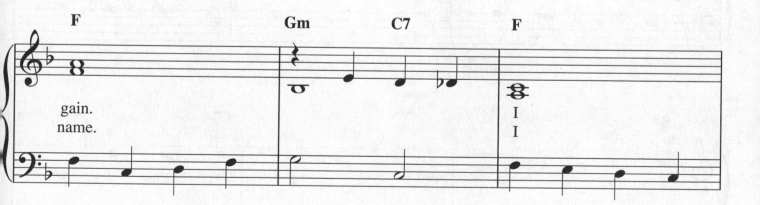

gain.
name.

fall_____ to piec - es,_____
fall____ to piec - es,_____

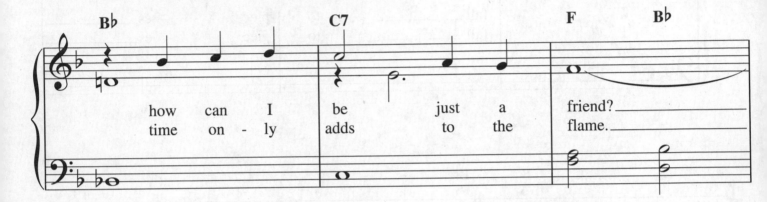

how can I be just a friend?_____
time on - ly adds to the flame._____

___ You want me to act like we've
___ You tell me to find some - one

nev - er kissed,_____ you want me to for -
else to love,_____ some - one who'll love me

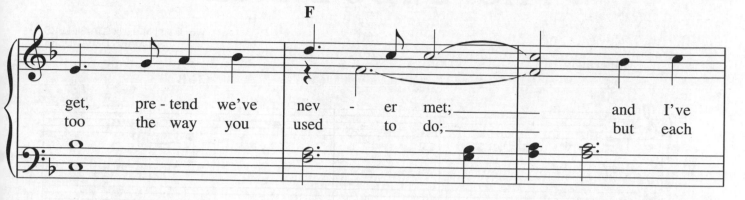

get,   pre - tend   we've   nev - er   met;_____   and   I've
too   the   way   you   used   to   do;_____   but   each

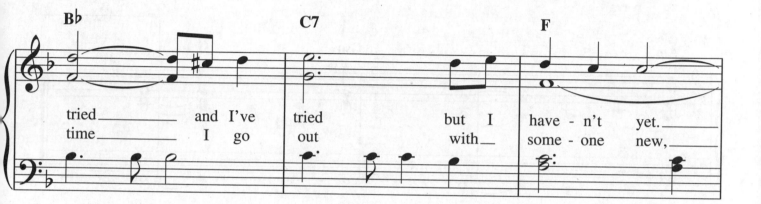

tried_____   and   I've   tried   but   I   have - n't   yet._____
time_____   I   go   out   with__   some - one   new,_____

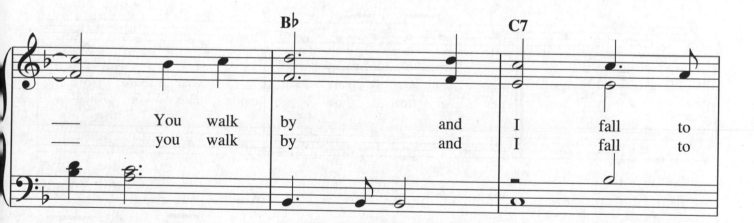

——   You   walk   by   and   I   fall   to
——   you   walk   by   and   I   fall   to

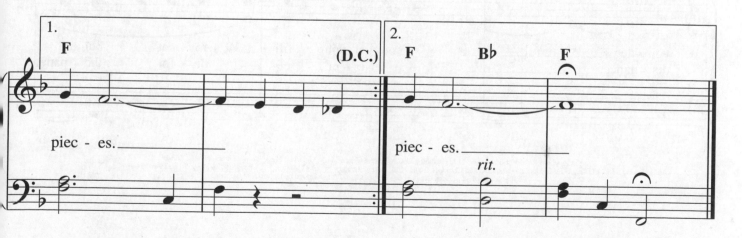

1.   piec - es._____   (D.C.)

2.   piec - es._____   rit.

I HOPE YOU DANCE

Words and Music by TIA SILLERS
and MARK D. SANDERS

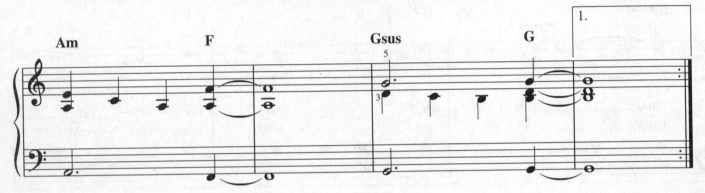

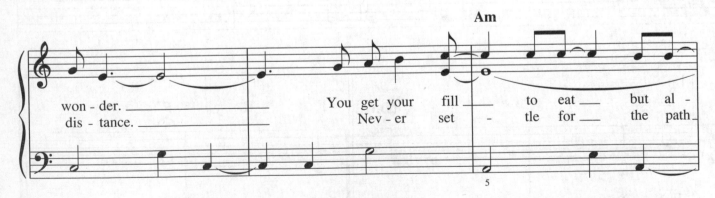

- ways   keep that   hun - ger._____   May you
_____ of   least   re - sist - ance._____   Liv - in'

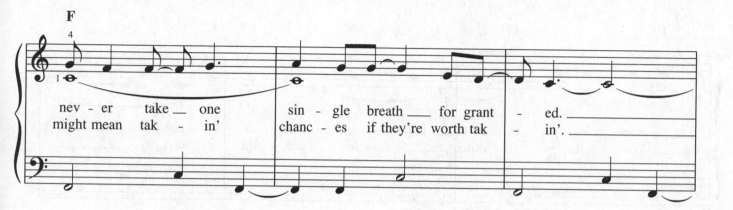

F

nev - er   take __ one   sin - gle   breath __ for grant - ed. _____
might mean   tak - in'   chanc - es   if they're worth tak - in'. _____

G

_____   God   for - bid ___ love   ev - er   leaves ___   you emp - ty - hand -
_____   Lov - in' might ___ be   a   mis - take ___   but it's ___ worth mak -

%

F   **G**

- ed. _____   I hope you   still __ feel   small _   when you
- in'. _____   Don't   let ___ some   hell - bent

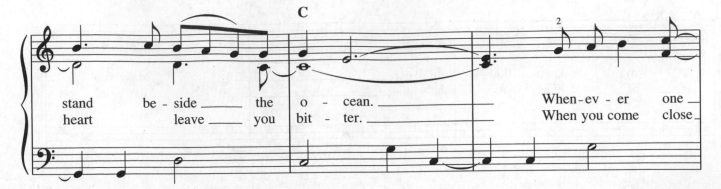

stand   be - side _____ the   o - cean.
heart   leave _____ you   bit - ter. _____

When-ev - er   one _____
When you come   close

_____ door   clos - es,   I _____   hope   one _ more   o - pens. _____
_____ to   sell - in' out, _____   re - con - sid - er. _____

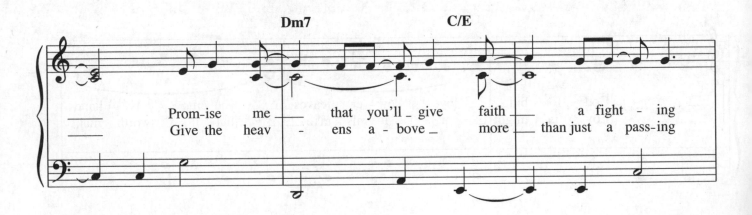

_____   Prom-ise   me _____   that you'll _ give   faith _____   a fight - ing
_____   Give the   heav - ens   a - bove _   more _____   than just   a pass-ing

To Coda

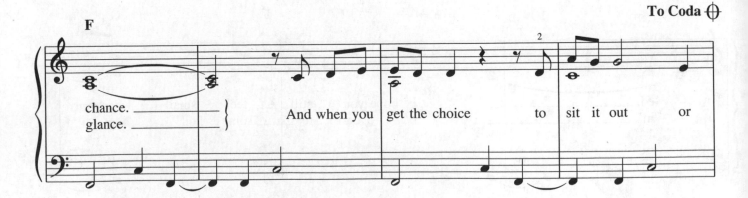

chance. _____
glance. _____

And when you   get the choice   to   sit it out   or

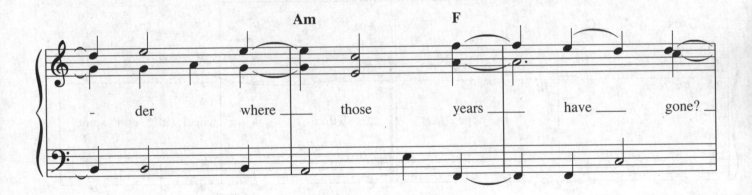

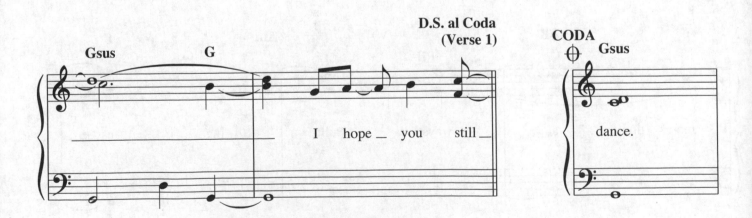

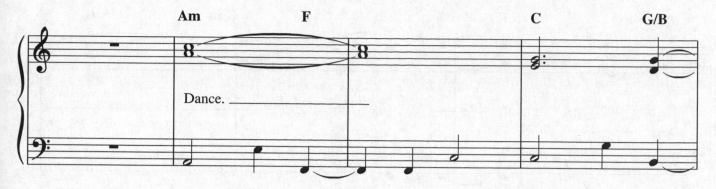

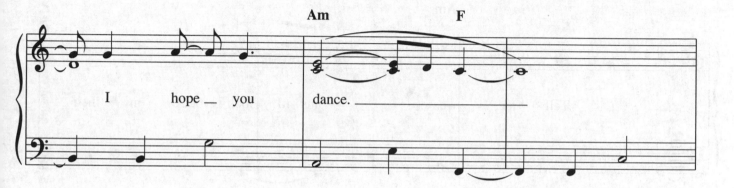

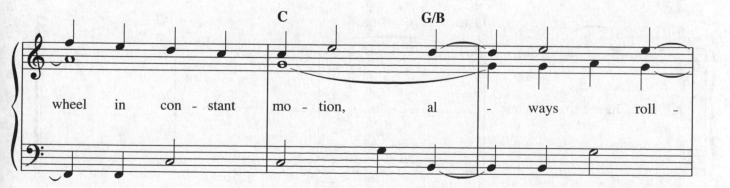

-ing us _____ a - long.

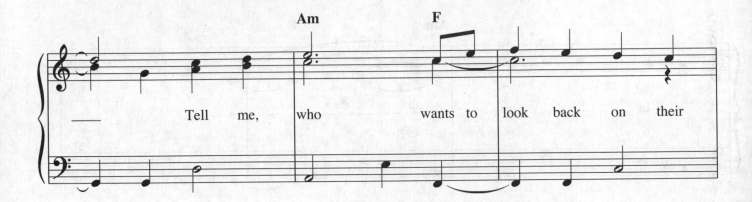

___ Tell me, who wants to look back on their

youth and won - der where ____ those years ___

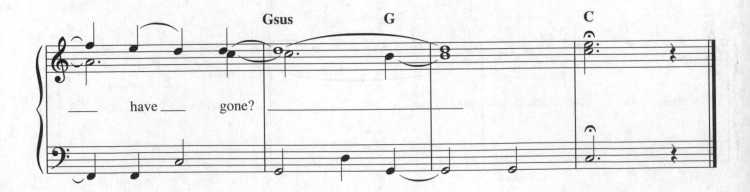

___ have ___ gone? _____

I'M SO LONESOME I COULD CRY

Words and Music by
HANK WILLIAMS

Moderately
F

mf

With pedal

Hear _____ that lone - some whip - poor - will, he
ev - er see _____ a rob - in weep when

sounds _____ too blue _____ to fly. _____ The
leaves _____ be - gan _____ to die? _____ That

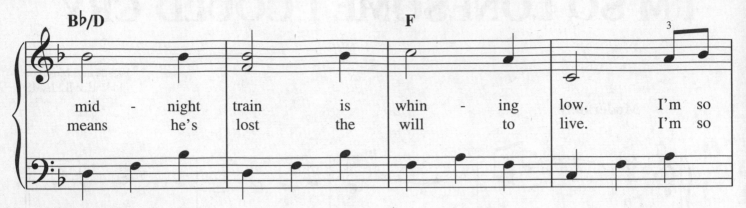

Bb/D **F**

mid - night train is whin - ing low. I'm so
means he's lost is the will to live. I'm so

C7/E **F**

lone - some I could _ cry._____ I've
lone - some I could _ cry._____ The

nev - er seen _____ a night _____ so
si - lence of _____ a fall - ing

long, when time _____ goes crawl - ing
star lights up _____ a pur - ple

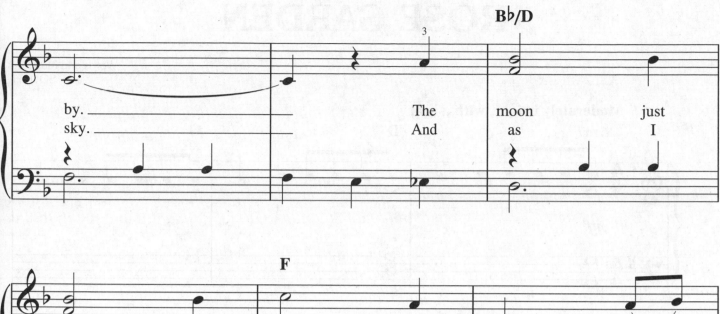

B♭/D

by. ____ The moon just
sky. ____ And as I

F

went be - hind a cloud to ____
won - der where you are I'm so

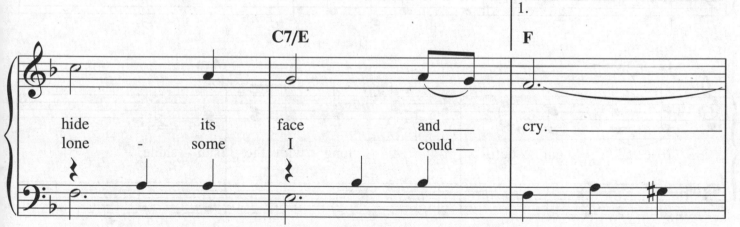

C7/E

hide its face and ____ cry. ____
lone - some I could ____

1.
F

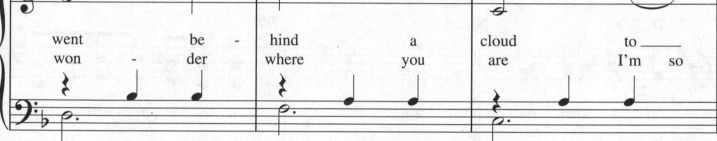

2.
F

Did you cry.
rit.

(I Never Promised You A)
ROSE GARDEN

Words and Music by
JOE SOUTH

Moderately bright, with a beat

I beg your par-don, I nev-er prom-ised you a

rose____ gar-den. A - long with the sun-shine,

there's got to be a lit-tle rain some-time.____ When you

take, you got to give, so live and let live __ or let go, oh, oh, oh. __

__ I beg your par - don, I nev - er prom ised you a

rose __ gar - den. __

I could prom-ise you things __ like
I could sing you a tune __ and

sweet talk - ing you __ could
look be - fore you leap, still

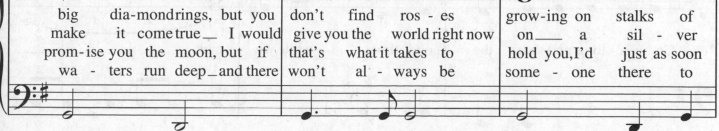

big dia-mond rings, but you don't find ros - es grow-ing on stalks of
make it come true __ I would give you the world right now on __ a sil - ver
prom-ise you the moon, but if that's what it takes to hold you, I'd just as soon
wa - ters run deep __ and there won't al - ways be some - one there to

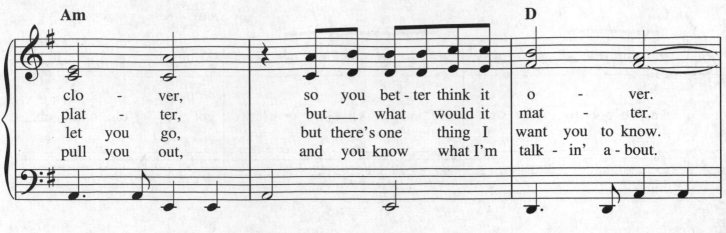

Am

clo - ver,
plat - ter,
let you go,
pull you out,

so you bet - ter think it o - ver.
but___ what would it mat - ter.
but there's one thing I want you to know.
and you know what I'm talk - in' a - bout.

D

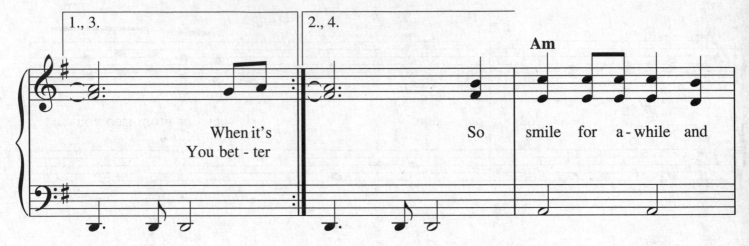

1., 3.

When it's
You bet - ter

2., 4.

So smile for a - while and

Am

D

let's be jol - ly;

Bdim

love should-n't be so

E7

mel - an - chol - y.

To Coda ⊕

Am

Come a - long and share the

good times while we

C

can.___

189

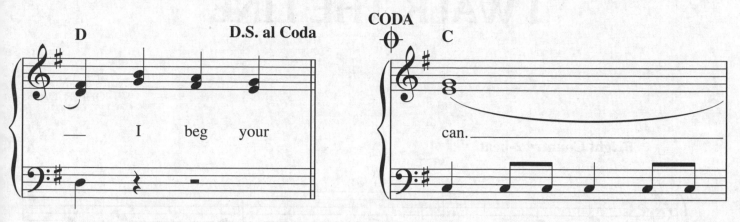

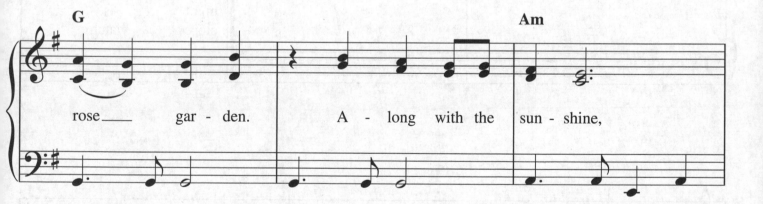

I WALK THE LINE

Words and Music by
JOHN R. CASH

C7   **F**

eyes	wide	o	-	pen	all	the	time.
on	my	mind	both	day	and	night.
eyes	wide	o	-	pen	all	the	time.

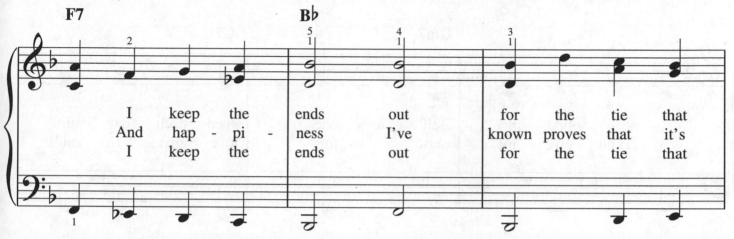

F7   **B♭**

I	keep	the	ends	out	for	the	tie	that
And	hap	-	pi	-	ness	I've	known	proves	that	it's
I	keep	the	ends	out	for	the	tie	that

F   **C7**

binds.	Be	-	cause	you're	mine
right.	Be	-	cause	you're	mine
binds.	Be	-	cause	you're	mine

To Coda   **F**   **B♭**   **C7**   **F**

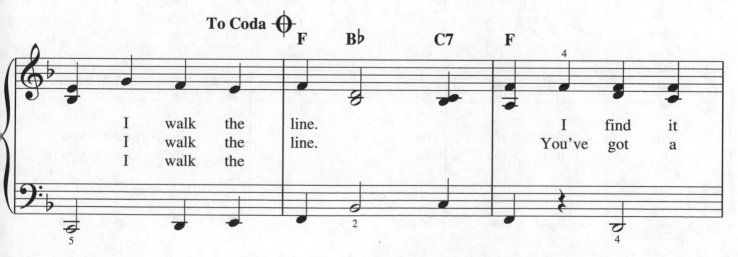

I	walk	the	line.			I	find	it
I	walk	the	line.			You've	got	a
I	walk	the						

ver - y   eas - y   to   be   true.
way   to   keep   me   on   your   side.

I   find   my - self   a - lone   when   each   day   is
You   give   me   cause   for   love   that   I   can't

through.   Yes,   I'll   ad - mit   that
hide.   For   you   I   know   I'd

I'm   a   fool   for   you.   Be - cause you're
e - ven turn the   tide.   Be - cause you're

mine   I   walk   the   line.
mine   I   walk   the

As   sure   as   line.   I   keep   a

CODA

line.   Be - cause you're   mine

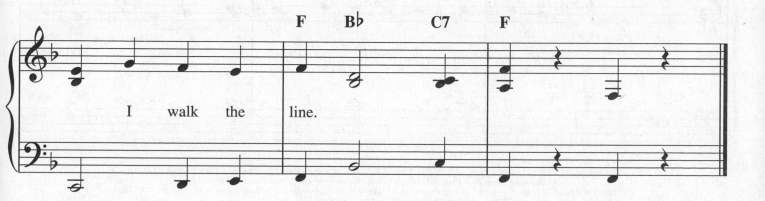

I   walk   the   line.

I'M ALREADY THERE

Words and Music by GARY BAKER,
FRANK MYERS and RICHIE McDONALD

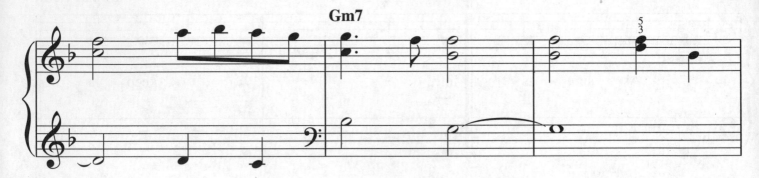

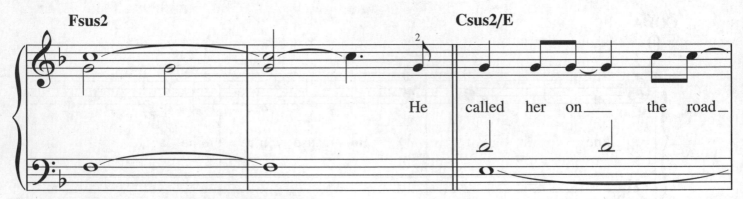

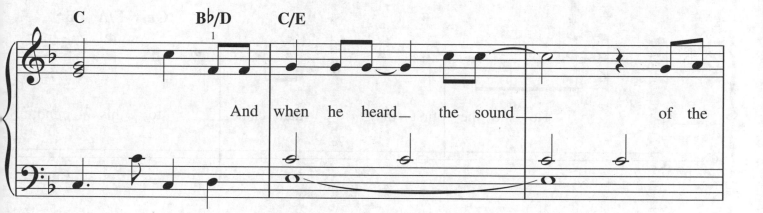

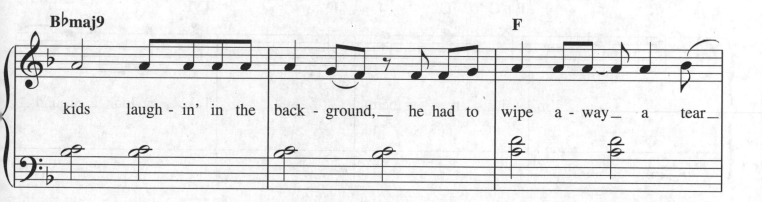

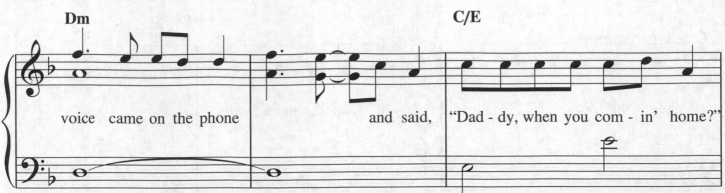

voice came on the phone and said, "Dad - dy, when you com - in' home?"

He said the first thing that came to his mind:

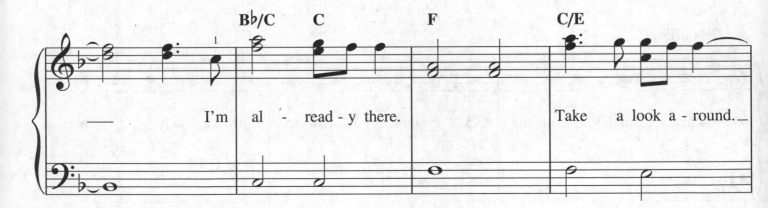

I'm al - read - y there. Take a look a - round.

I'm the sun - shine in your hair, I'm the

shad - ow on the ground. I'm the whis - per in the wind,

I'm your i - mag - i - nar - y friend.

And I know I'm in your prayers. Oh, I'm

al - read - y there.

She got back on___ the phone said, "I

real - ly miss_ you, dar - lin'._ Don't_ wor - ry a - bout_ the kids,_

___ they'll be___ al - right.___ I wish

I was in___ your arms,___ ly - in' right there_ be - side_

you.— But I know that I'll— be in your dreams_ to - night._

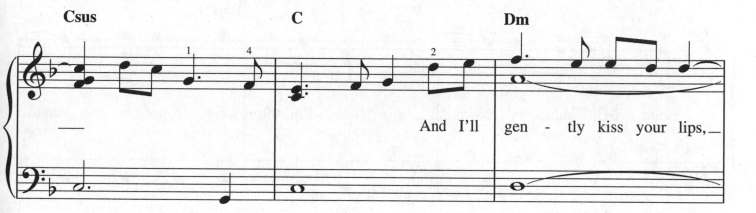

Csus **C** **Dm**

— And I'll gen - tly kiss your lips,—

C/E **F**

— touch you with my fin-ger-tips.— So, turn out the light

Gm F/A B♭ **B♭/C** **C** **F**

and close your eyes.——— I'm al - read-y there.—

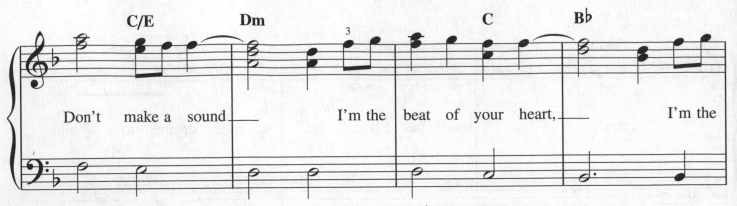

Don't make a sound — I'm the beat of your heart, — I'm the

moon - light shin - in' down. — I'm the whis - per in the wind, —

— and I'll be there till the end. —

Can you feel — the love that we've shared? — Oh, I'm

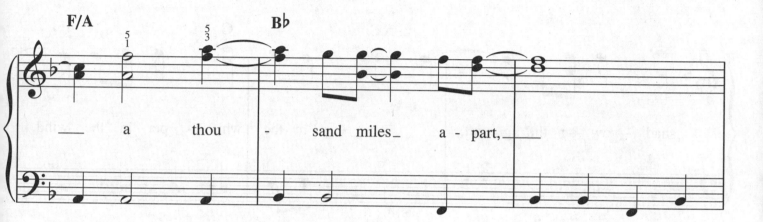

Dm7

B♭sus2

I'm the sun - shine in your hair, I'm the

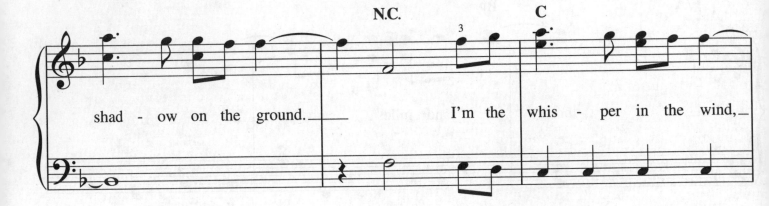

N.C.

C

shad - ow on the ground. I'm the whis - per in the wind,

F

C/E

Dm7

and I'll be there till the end.

Am7

Can you feel the love that we've shared?

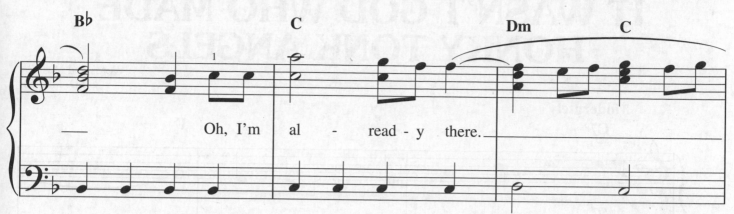

IT WASN'T GOD WHO MADE HONKY TONK ANGELS

Words and Music by
J.D. MILLER

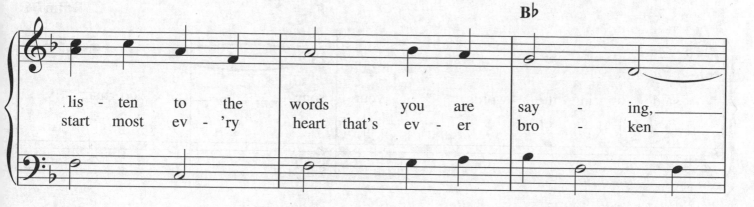

listen to the words you are say - ing, ____
start most ev - 'ry heart that's ev - er bro - ken ____

____ it brings mem - 'ries when I was a trust - ing
____ was be - cause there al - ways was a man to

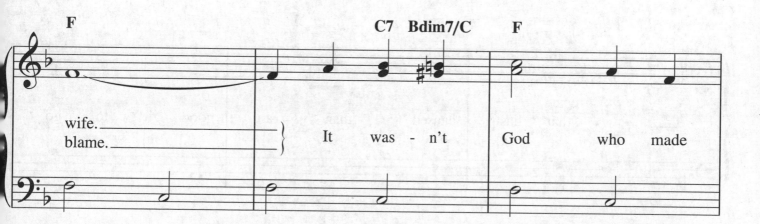

wife. ____ It was - n't God who made
blame. ____

hon - ky tonk an - gels, ____ as you

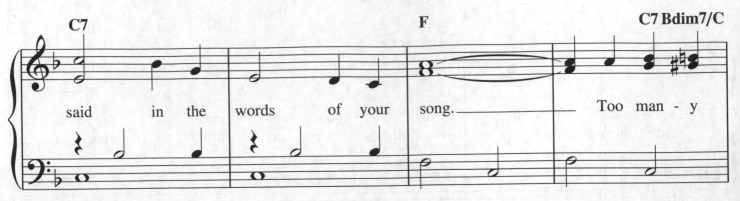

said in the words of your song._____ Too man - y

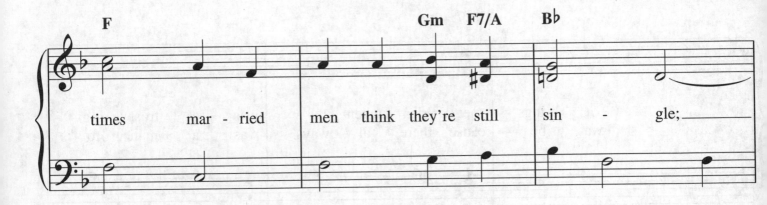

times mar - ried men think they're still sin - gle;_____

_____ that has caused man - y a good girl to go

1.

wrong._____ It's a

2.

wrong._____

KING OF THE ROAD

Words and Music by
ROGER MILLER

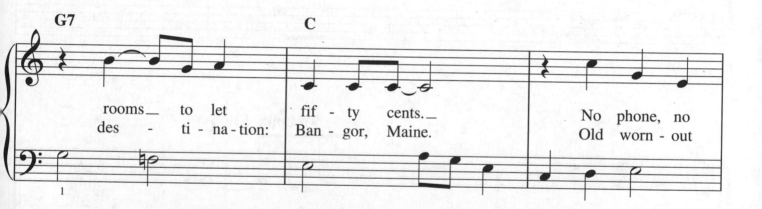

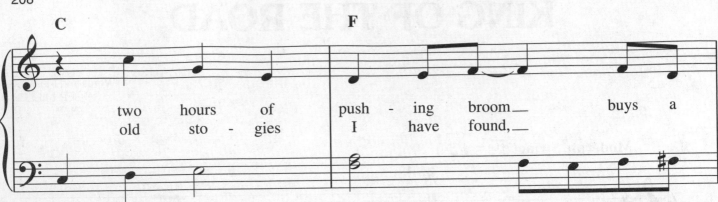

two hours of | push - ing broom___ buys a
old sto - gies | I have found,___

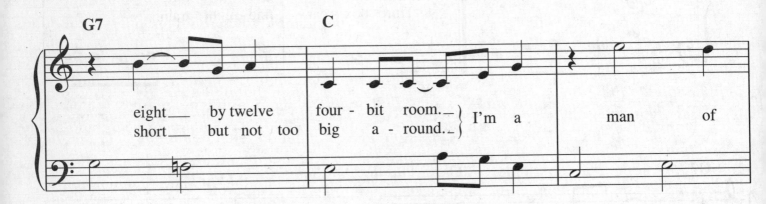

eight___ by twelve | four - bit room.___ I'm a | man of
short___ but not too | big a - round.___

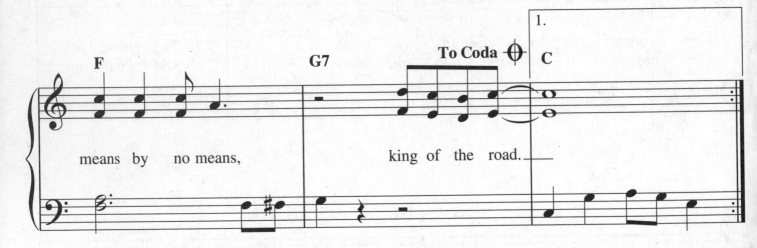

means by no means, | king of the road.___

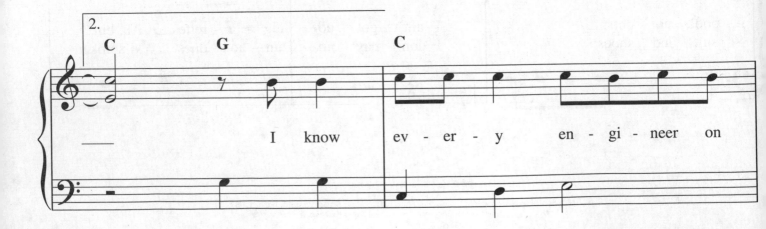

___ I know | ev - er - y en - gi - neer on

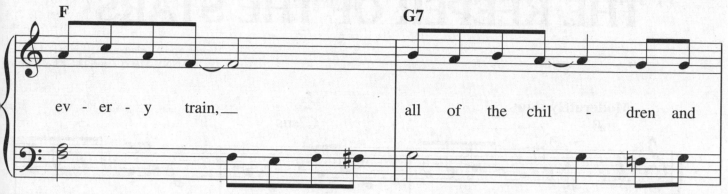

ev - er - y train,___ all of the chil - dren and

all of their names,___ and ev - er - y hand - out in

ev - er - y town,___ and ev - 'ry lock that ain't locked when

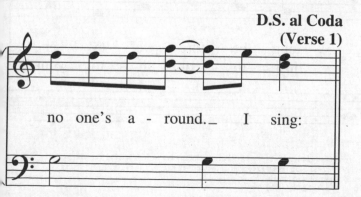

D.S. al Coda
(Verse 1)

no one's a - round.___ I sing:

CODA

THE KEEPER OF THE STARS

Words and Music by KAREN STALEY,
DANNY MAYO and DICKEY LEE

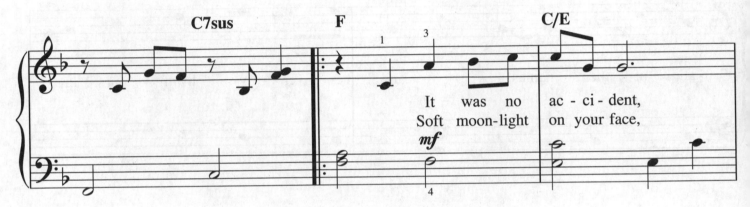

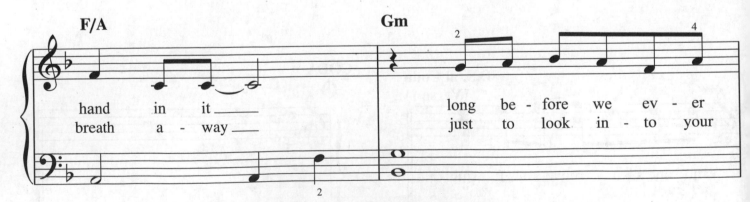

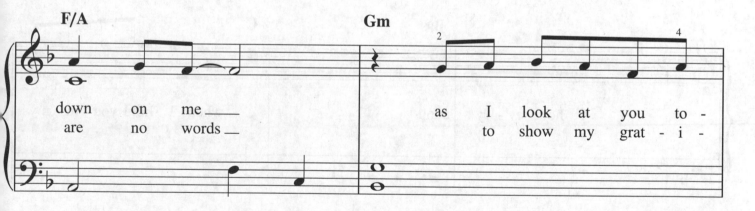

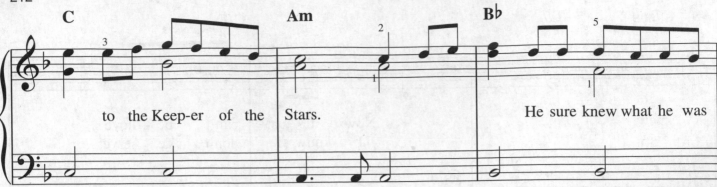

to the Keep-er of the Stars. He sure knew what he was

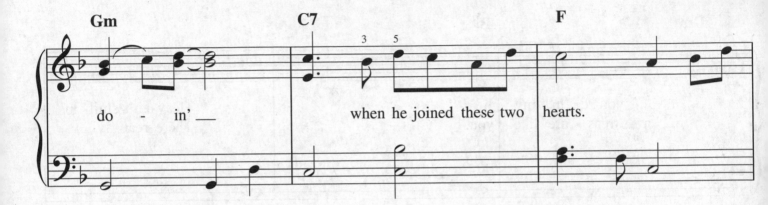

do - in' ___ when he joined these two hearts.

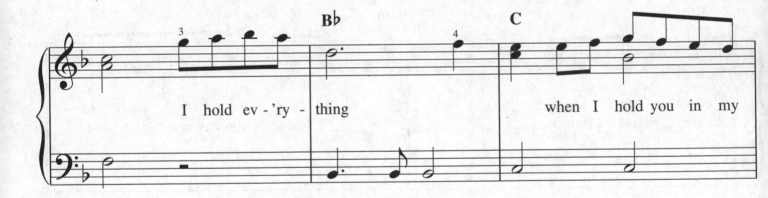

I hold ev-'ry - thing when I hold you in my

arms. I've got all I'll ev - er need,

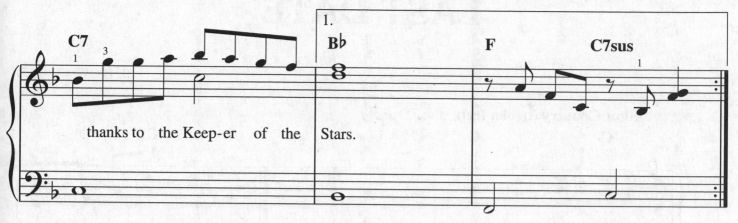

thanks to the Keep-er of the Stars.

Stars.   It was no ac - ci dent,

me find-ing you.   Some - one had a

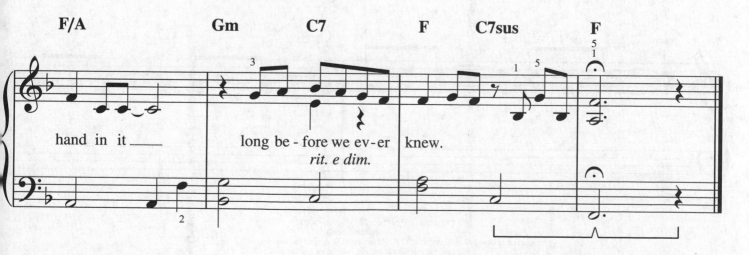

hand in it ____   long be - fore we ev - er knew.

rit. e dim.

LAST DATE

By FLOYD CRAMER

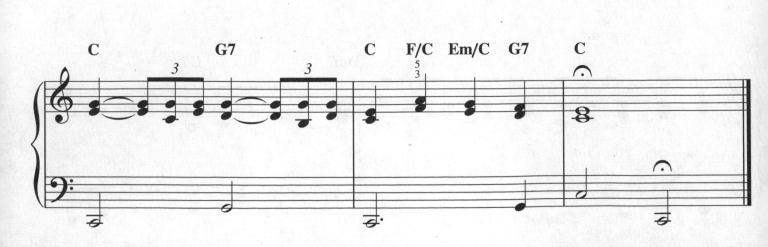

LOVE STORY

Words and Music by
TAYLOR SWIFT

218

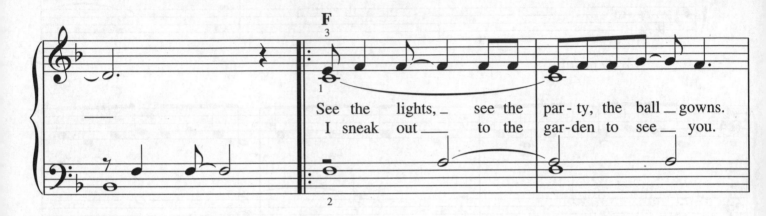

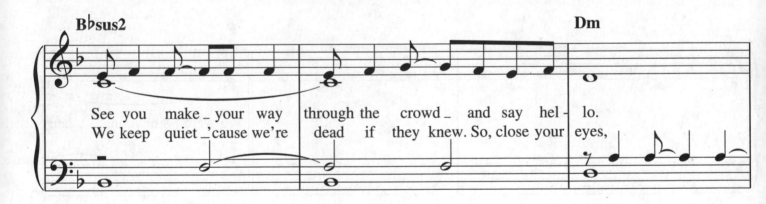

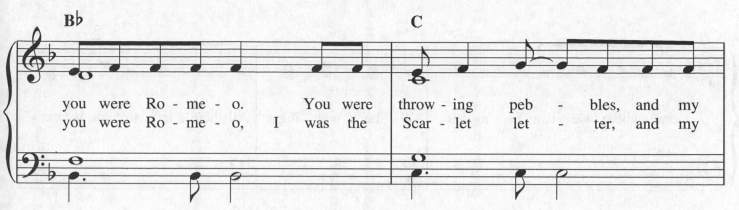

B♭

you were Ro - me - o. You were
you were Ro - me - o, I was the

C

throw - ing peb - bles, and my
Scar - let let - ter, and my

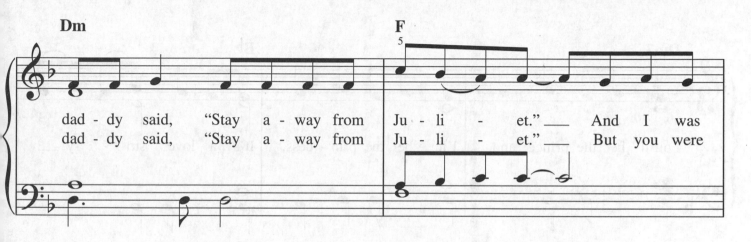

Dm

dad - dy said, "Stay a - way from
dad - dy said, "Stay a - way from

F

Ju - li - et." ___ And I was
Ju - li - et." ___ But you were

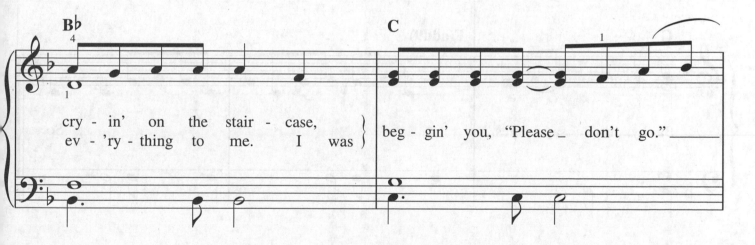

B♭

cry - in' on the stair - case,
ev - 'ry - thing to me. I was

C

beg - gin' you, "Please ___ don't go." ___

Dm

___

B♭ **Csus**

And I ___ said,

F

"Ro - me - o, take me

220

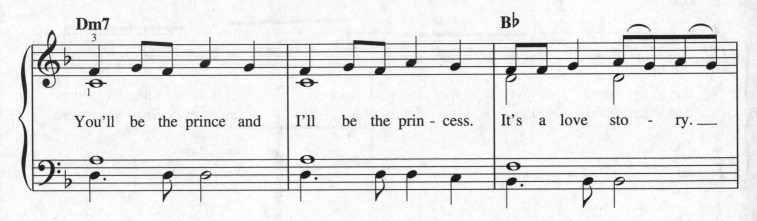

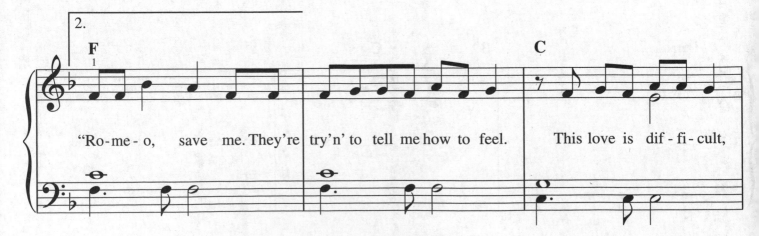

but it's _ real. _ Don't be a-fraid. We'll make it out of this mess.

It's a love sto - ry. _ Ba - by, just say _ yes." _ I got tired of

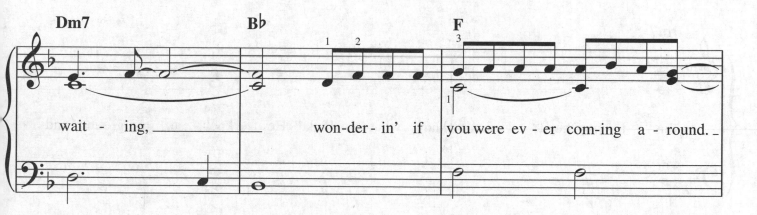

wait - ing, _____ won-der - in' if you were ev - er com-ing a - round. _

_ My faith in you was fad - ing _____ when I

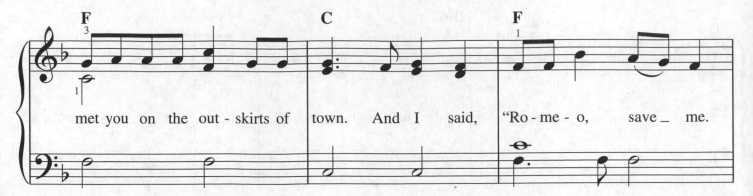

met you on the out - skirts of town. And I said, "Ro - me - o, save _ me.

I've been feel - in' so a - lone. I keep wait - ing for you, but you nev - er come. Is

this in my head? I don't know what to think." He knelt to the ground and

pulled out a ring and said, "Mar - ry me, Ju - li - et, you nev - er have to be a - lone.

I love you __ and that's all I real-ly know. I talked to your dad. Go

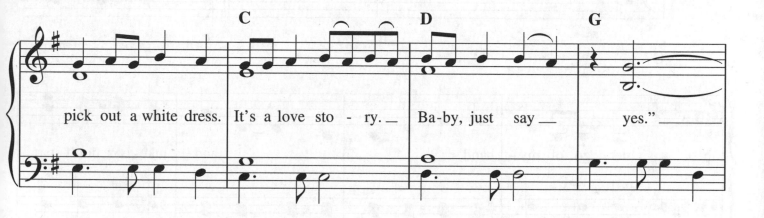

pick out a white dress. It's a love sto - ry. __ Ba-by, just say __ yes." __

__ Oh, oh, oh, _____ oh, oh, oh, oh.

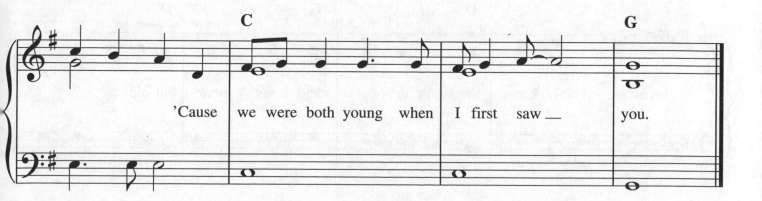

'Cause we were both young when I first saw __ you.

LONGNECK BOTTLE

Words and Music by RICK CARNES
and STEVE WARINER

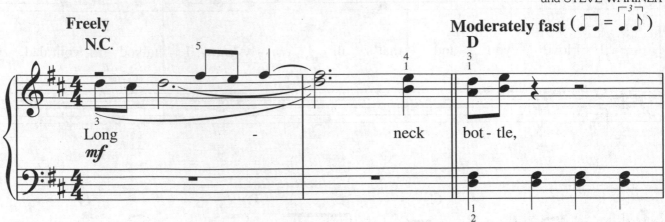

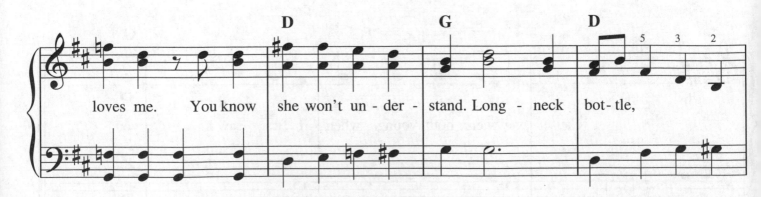

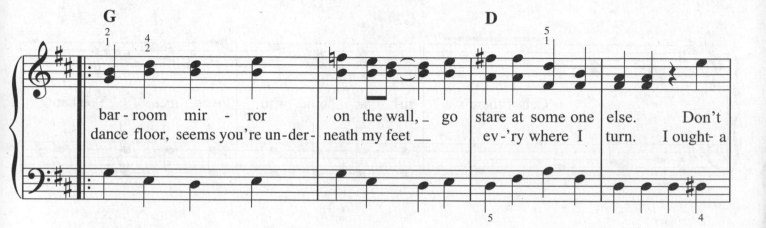

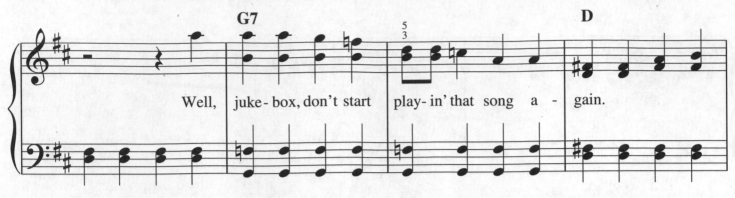

Well, juke-box, don't start play-in' that song a-gain.

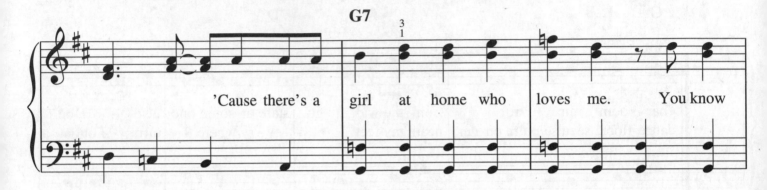

'Cause there's a girl at home who loves me. You know

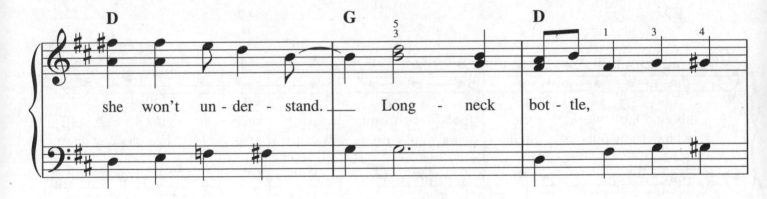

she won't un-der-stand. Long-neck bot-tle,

let go of my hand. Hey,

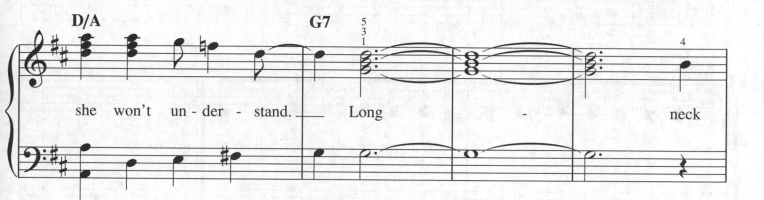

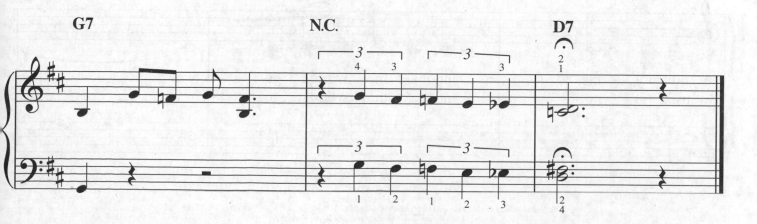

MAKE THE WORLD GO AWAY

Words and Music by
HANK COCHRAN

Make the world go a - way, and get it off___ my___

shoul - ders. Say the things you used to say,

1.

and make the world___ go a - way._____ I'm sor - ry if I

2.

and make the world___ go a - way.

rit.

MAMMAS DON'T LET YOUR BABIES GROW UP TO BE COWBOYS

Words and Music by ED BRUCE
and PATSY BRUCE

let 'em   pick   gui - tars   and   drive   them   old

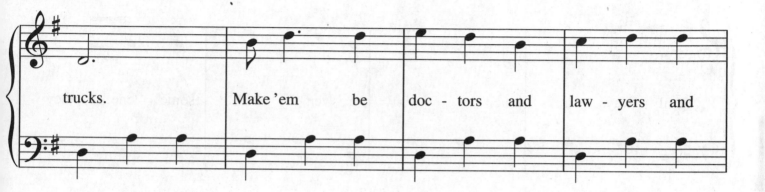

trucks.   Make 'em   be   doc - tors   and   law - yers   and

such.   Mam - mas,_____   don't   let   your

ba - bies   grow   up___ to   be   cow - boys,

D7   **D**

'cause they'll nev - er stay — home, and they're

al - ways a - lone, e - ven with some - one — they

G   **D**

love.   A

                                                      A

G   **G7**

cow-boy ain't eas - y to love and he's hard - er — to
cow-boy loves smok - y ole pool rooms and clear moun - tain

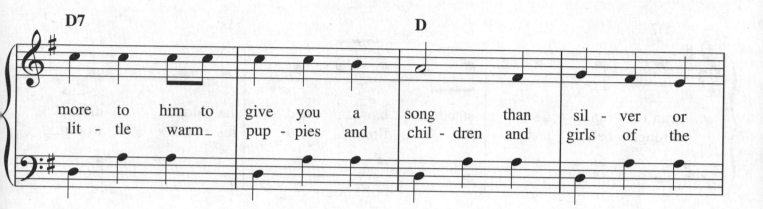

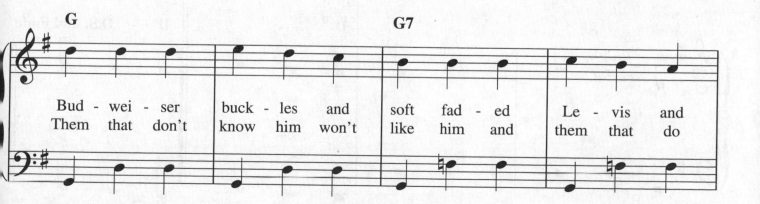

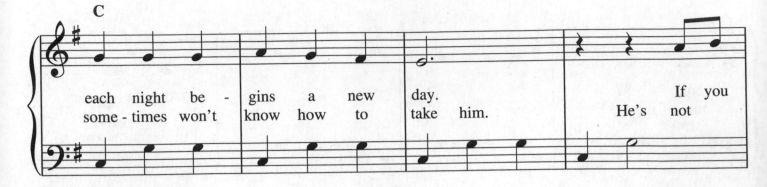

each night be - gins a new day.   He's not
some - times won't know how to take him.

can't un - der - stand___ him___ and   he don't   die___
wrong, he's just dif - f'rent___ and   his pride   won't___

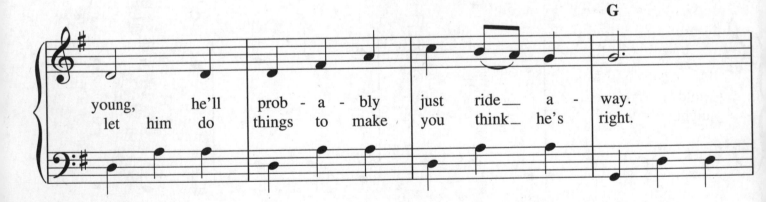

young, he'll prob - a - bly just ride___ a - way.
let him do things to make you think___ he's right.

NEED YOU NOW

Words and Music by HILLARY SCOTT,
CHARLES KELLEY, DAVE HAYWOOD
and JOSH KEAR

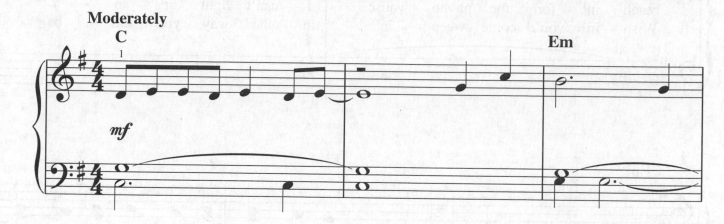

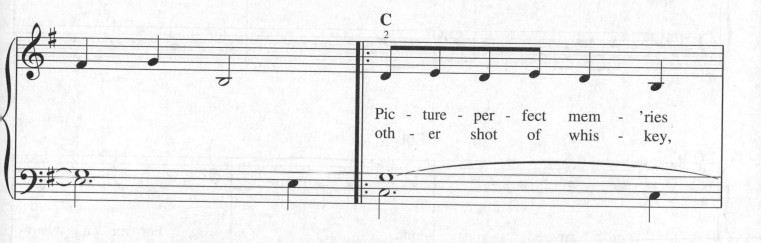

Pic - ture - per - fect mem - 'ries
oth - er shot of whis - key,

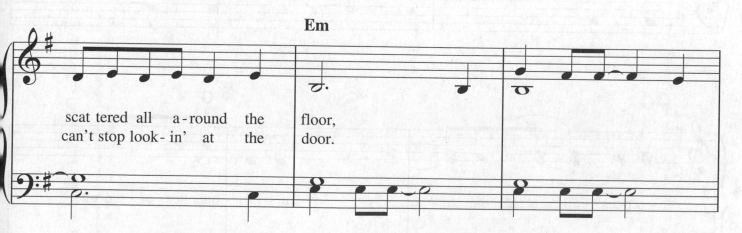

scat tered all a-round the floor,
can't stop look-in' at the door.

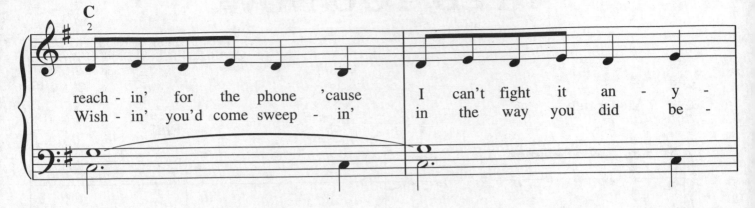

reach - in' for the phone 'cause
Wish - in' you'd come sweep - in'

I can't fight it an - y -
in the way you did be -

more.
fore.

And I won - der if __ I ev -

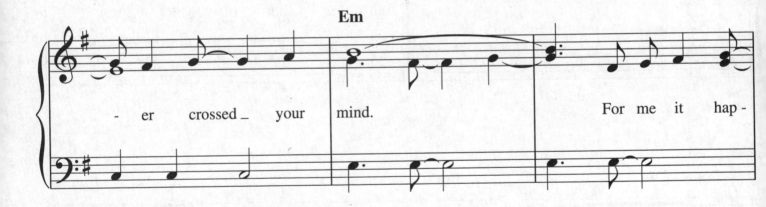

- er crossed __ your mind.

For me it hap -

- pens all __ the time. __

It's a quar-ter af - ter one,

score="1"237

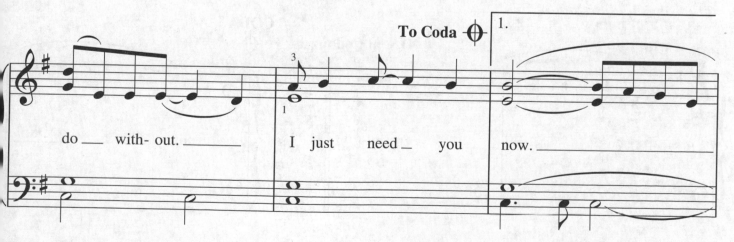

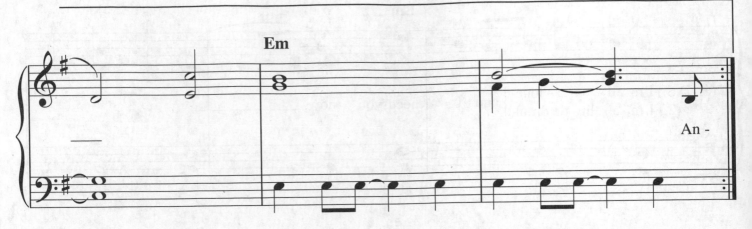

Em

2.

Em   **D**   **G**   **C**

now.

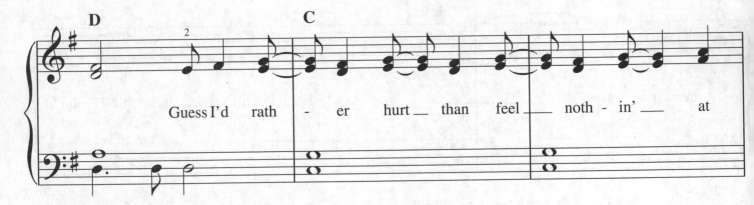

D   **C**

Guess I'd rath - er hurt __ than feel __ noth - in' __ at

Em   **D**   **D.S. al Coda**

all. __   It's a

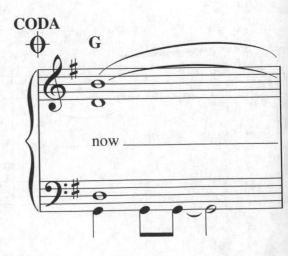

CODA

G

now __

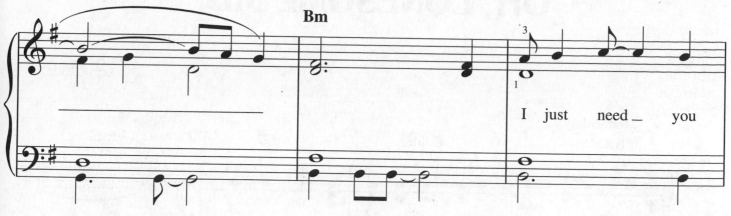

I just need ___ you

now. _____ Oh, ___

ba - by, I need ___ you now. _____

OH, LONESOME ME

Words and Music by
DON GIBSON

Ev - 'ry - bod - y's go - in' out and hav - in' fun;
bad mis - take I'm mak - in' by just hang - in' 'round;

I'm just a fool for stay - in' home and hav - in' none.
I know that I should have some fun and paint the town.

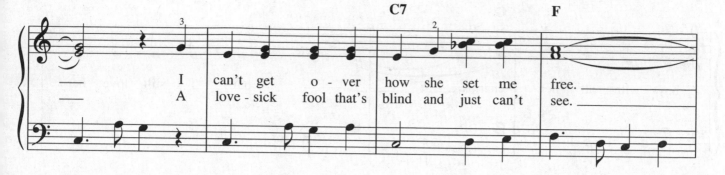

I can't get o-ver how she set me free. _____
A love-sick fool that's blind and just can't see. _____

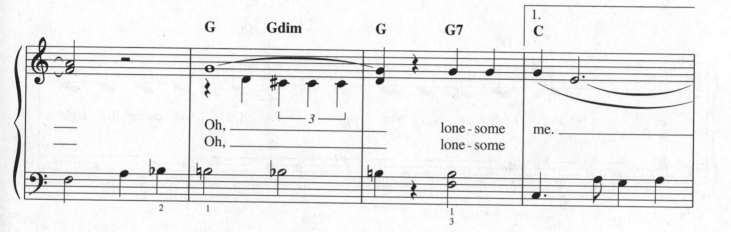

Oh, _____ lone-some me.
Oh, _____ lone-some

A me. _____ I'll bet she's not like

me; she's out and fan-cy-free, flirt-ing with the

boys with all her charms, _____ but I still love her

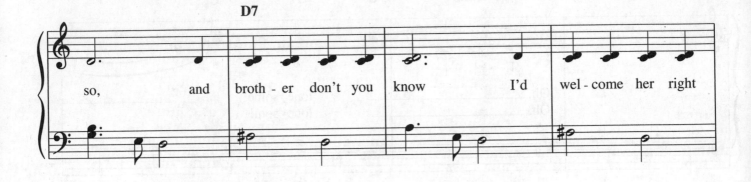

so, and broth - er don't you know I'd wel - come her right

back here in my arms. __ Well, there must be some way

I can lose these lone - some blues, _____ for - get a - bout the

243

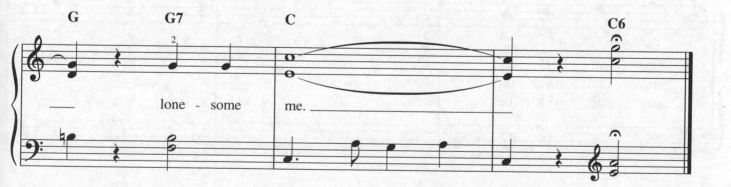

OKIE FROM MUSKOGEE

Words and Music by MERLE HAGGARD
and ROY EDWARD BURRIS

Moderately fast

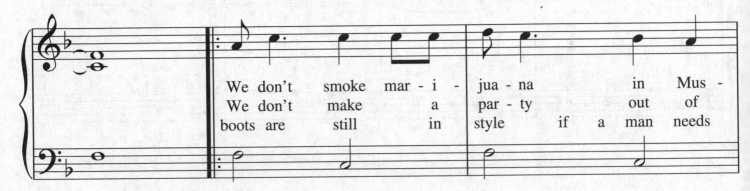

We don't smoke mar - i - jua - na in Mus -
We don't make a par - ty out of
boots are still in style if a man needs

ko - gee,_____ and we don't take our
lov - ing,_____ but we like hold - ing
foot - wear;_____ beads and Ro - man

trips on L. S. D.
hands and pitch - ing woo. And
san - dals won't be seen.

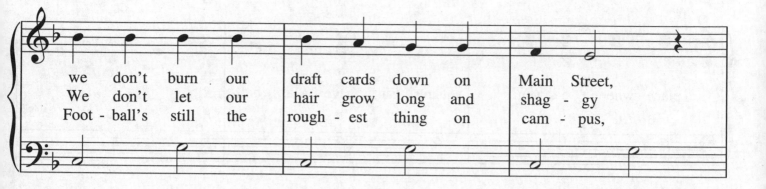

we don't burn our draft cards down on Main Street,
We don't let our hair grow long and shag - gy
Foot - ball's still the rough - est thing on cam - pus,

but we like liv - ing right and be - ing
like the hip - pies out in San Fran - cis - co
and the kids here still re - spect the col - lege

F

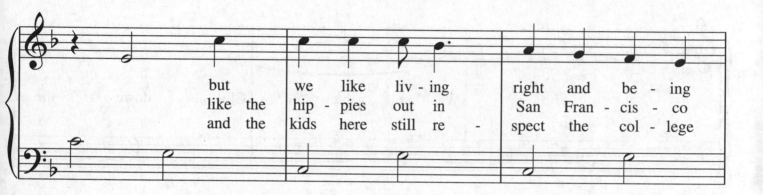

free.
do.
dean.

And I'm proud to be an

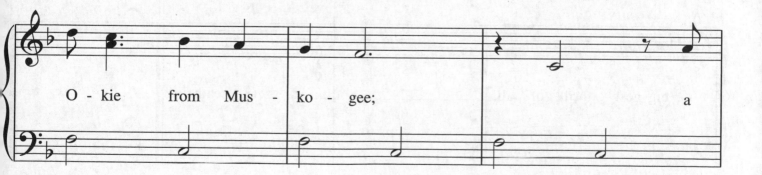

O - kie from Mus - ko - gee;

a

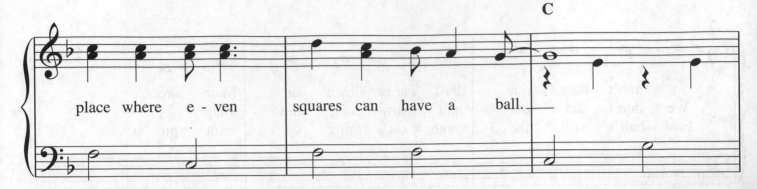

place where e - ven squares can have a ball. ___

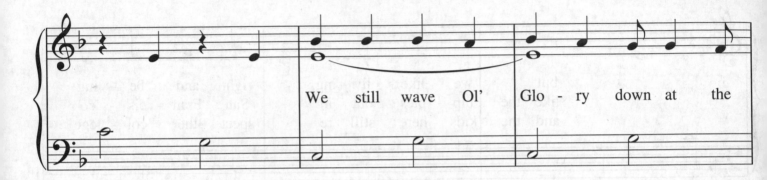

We still wave Ol' Glo - ry down at the

court - house, white light - ning's still the

big-gest thrill of all. ___ (3.) Leath-er

OUT LAST NIGHT

Words and Music by KENNY CHESNEY
and BRETT JAMES

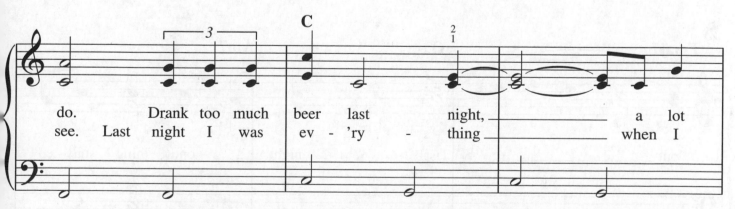

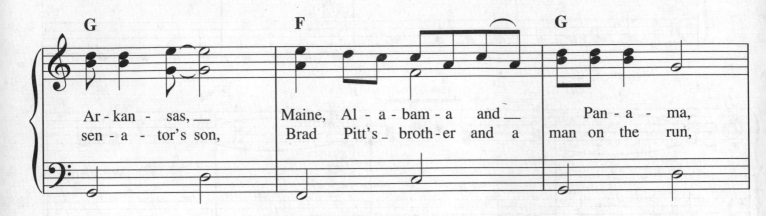

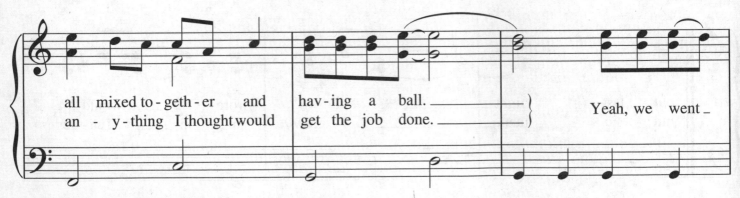

lead - ing to an - oth - er. Out _____ last

night,

{ hit - ting on ev - 'ry - bod - y and their moth - er. There were
hit - ting on ev - 'ry - bod - y and their moth - er. There were
ev - 'ry - bod - y start - ed lov - ing on each oth - er. They were }

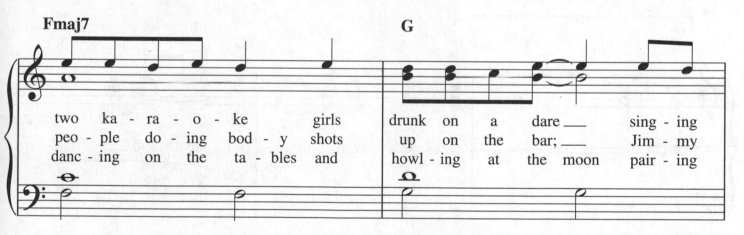

two ka - ra - o - ke girls drunk on a dare ___ sing - ing
peo - ple do - ing bod - y shots up on the bar; ___ Jim - my
danc - ing on the ta - bles and howl - ing at the moon pair - ing

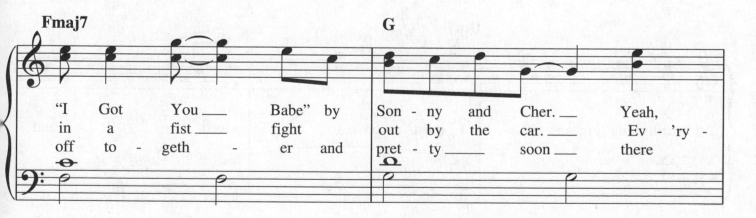

"I Got You ___ Babe" by Son - ny and Cher. ___ Yeah,
in a fist ___ fight out by the car. ___ Ev - 'ry -
off to - geth - er and pret - ty ___ soon ___ there

Fmaj7   G   **To Coda** ⊕

life was good ev - 'ry where.___ We went out___ last
bod - y was some___ kind of star___ when we went out last
was not a soul___ in sight___ when we went out last

1.
C   F

night.___ Well, you know I'm a

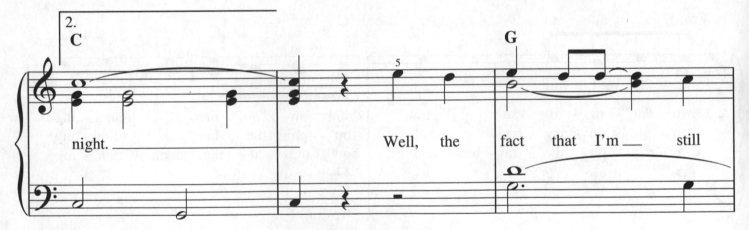

2.
C   G

night.___ Well, the fact that I'm___ still

Dm7

breath - ing means that I must have___ sur - vived,___ and

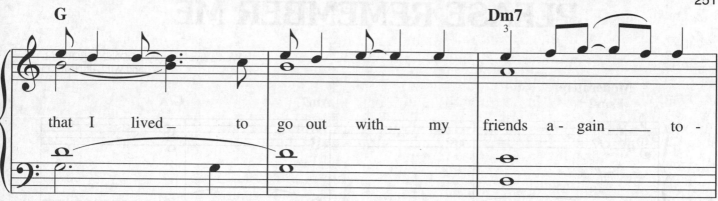

that I lived __ to go out with __ my friends a - gain ____ to -

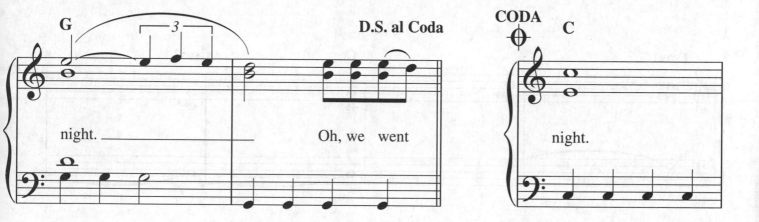

night. _____   Oh, we went   night.

rit.

PLEASE REMEMBER ME

Words and Music by RODNEY CROWELL
and WILL JENNINGS

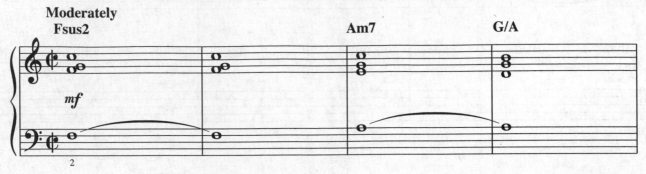

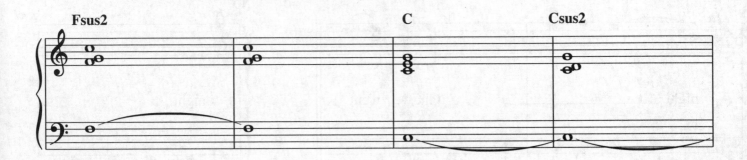

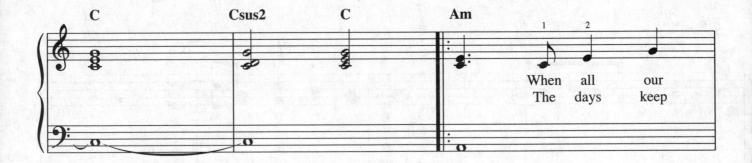

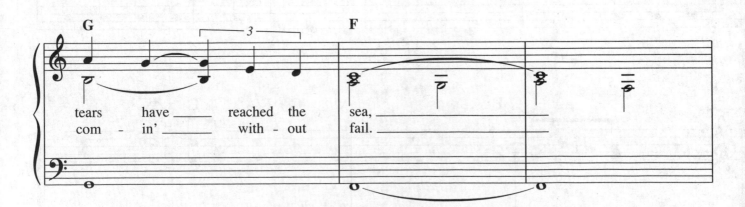

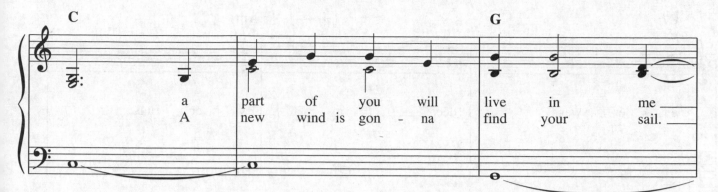

a part of you will live in me ___
A new wind is gon - na find your sail. ___

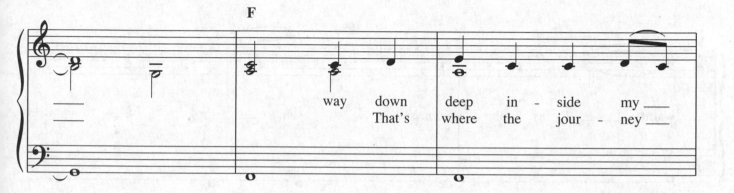

___ way down deep in - side my ___
___ That's where the jour - ney ___

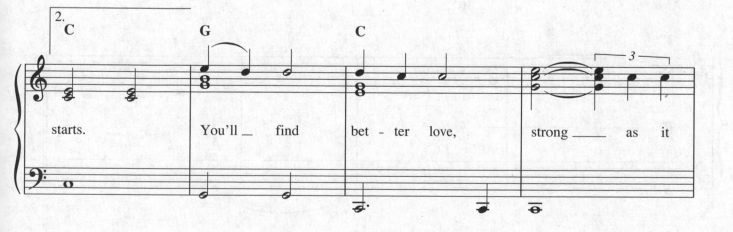

1.

heart. ___

2.

starts. You'll ___ find bet - ter love, strong ___ as it

ev - er was, deep _____ as a riv - er runs,

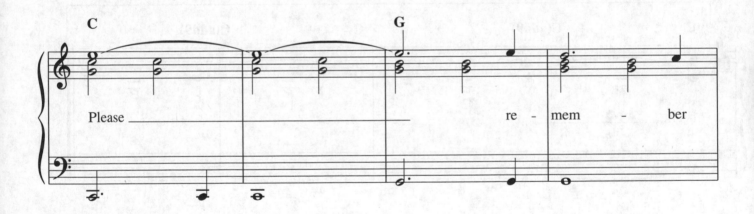

warm _____ as the morn - ing sun. _____

Please _____ re - mem - ber

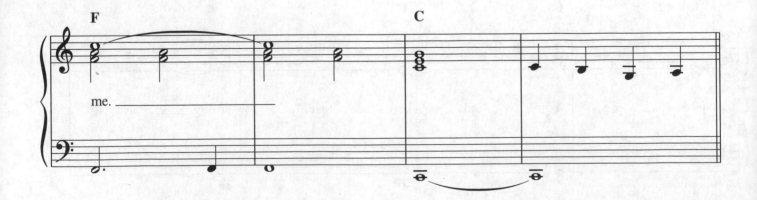

me. _____

Just like the waves down ___ by the shore, ___
Out in this brave new ___ world you'll see, ___

we're gon - na keep on com - in'
oh, the val - leys

back for more ___
and for the peaks. ___

'cause we don't
And I can

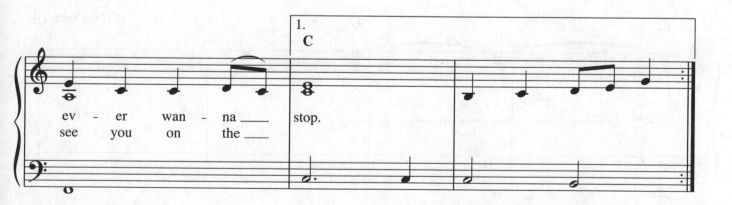

1.
C

ev - er wan - na ___ stop.
see you on the ___

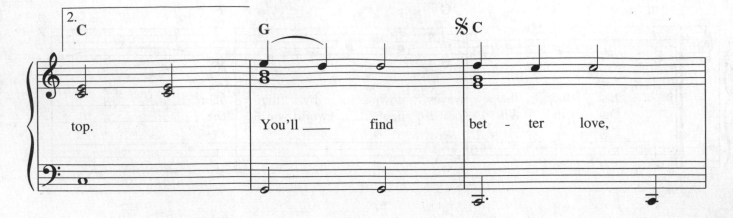

top. You'll ___ find bet - ter love,

strong ___ as it ev - er was, deep ___ as a

riv - er runs, warm ___ as the morn - ing sun. ___ Please

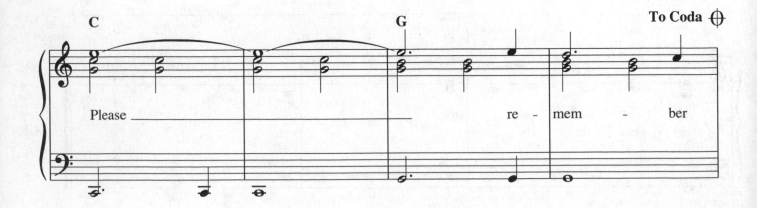

Please ___ re - mem - ber

To Coda ⊕

me.

Re - mem - ber me when you're out walk - ing,

when snow falls high out - side your door,

late at night when you're not sleep - in' _____

and moon - light falls a - cross your

floor

and I can't

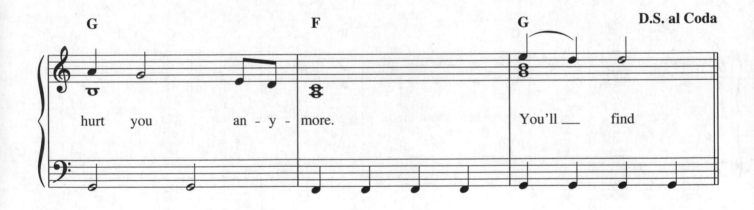

hurt you an - y - more.

You'll __ find

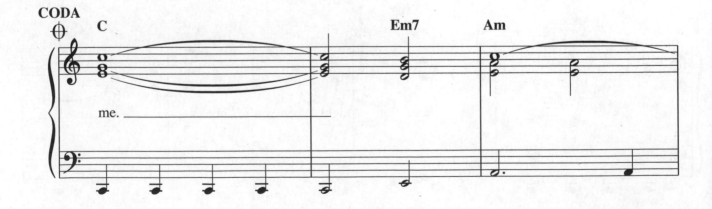

me.

Please _____

_____ re - mem - ber me. _____

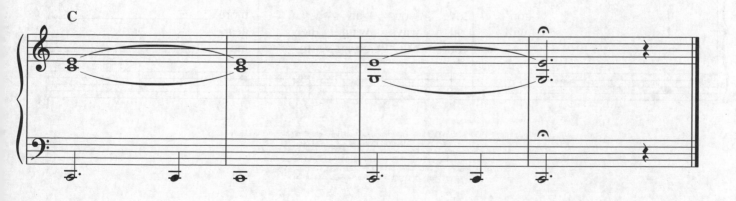

RELEASE ME

Words and Music by ROBERT YOUNT,
EDDIE MILLER and DUB WILLIAMS

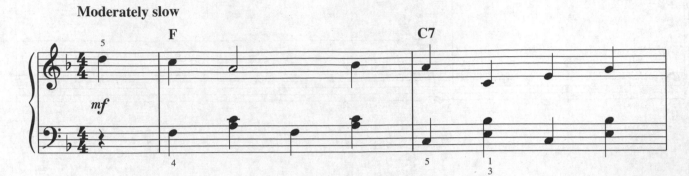

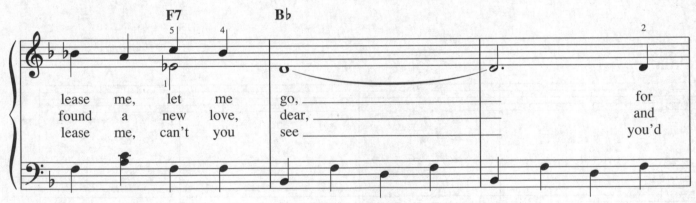

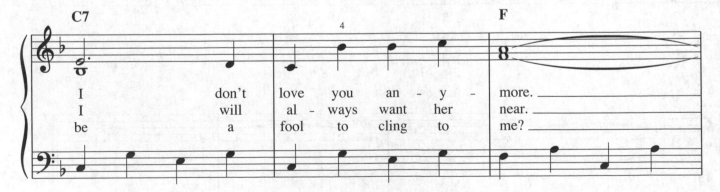

To waste our
Her lips are
To live a

F7   **B♭**

lives would be a sin; _____ re -
warm while yours are cold; _____ re -
lie would bring us pain, _____ so re -

F   **C7**   **1., 2.** **F**

lease me and let me love a - gain. _____
lease me, my dar - ling, let me go. _____
lease me and let me love a -

3.
F   **B♭/F**   **F**

gain. _____

SINGING THE BLUES

Words and Music by
MELVIN ENDSLEY

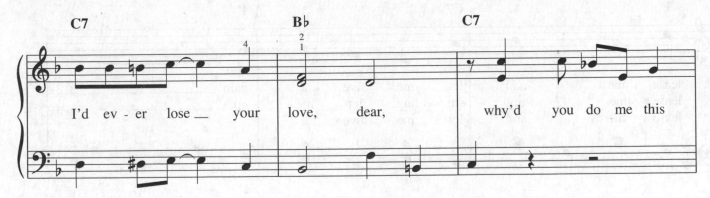

cry-ing all night _ 'cause ev-'ry-thing's wrong _ and noth-ing ain't right _ with-

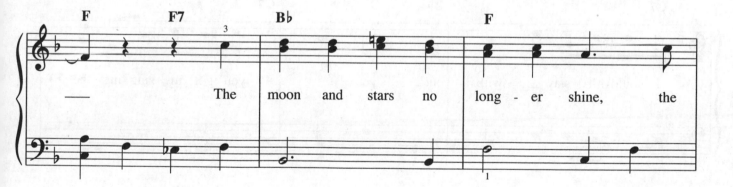

out you you got me sing-ing the blues. ____

— The moon and stars no long-er shine, the

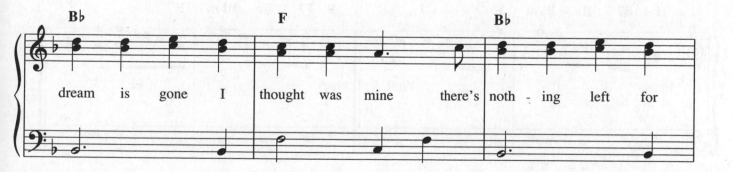

dream is gone I thought was mine there's noth-ing left for

me to do but cry _____ o - ver you. _ Well, I

nev - er felt more like run-ning a - way _ but why should I go _ 'cause

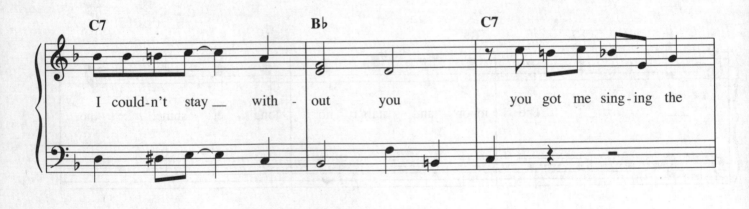

I could-n't stay _ with - out you you got me sing-ing the

1.
blues. Well, I

2.
blues.

SWEET DREAMS

Words and Music by
DON GIBSON

Sweet _____ dreams of you _____ ev - 'ry
Sweet _____ dreams of you, _____ things I

night _____ I go through. _____ Why
know _____ can't come true. _____ Why

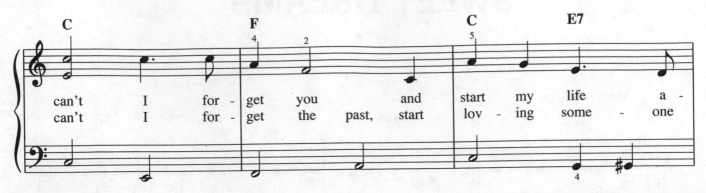

can't   I   for - get   you   and   start   my   life   a -
can't   I   for - get   you   the   past,   start   lov - ing   some - one

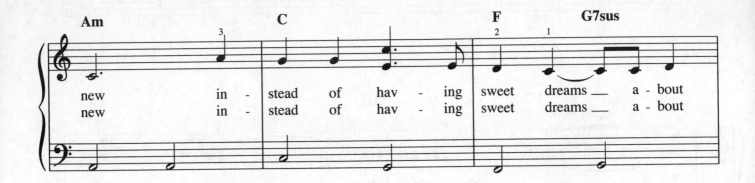

new   in - stead   of   hav - ing   sweet   dreams __   a - bout
new   in - stead   of   hav - ing   sweet   dreams __   a - bout

you?
you?   You   don't

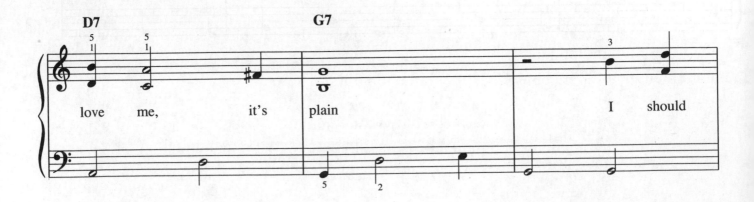

love   me,   it's   plain   I   should

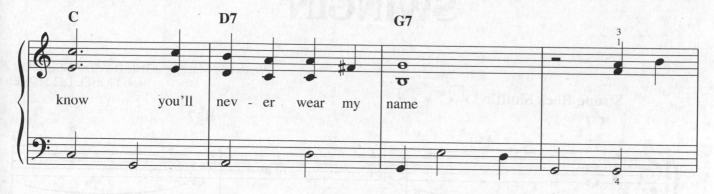

know　　you'll　nev - er　wear　my　name

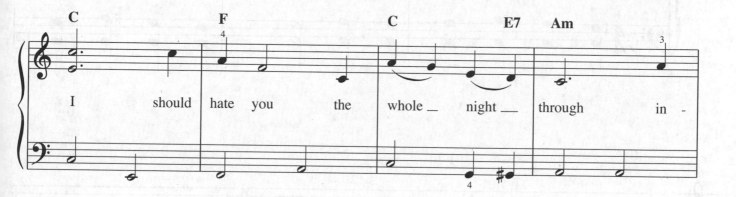

I　　should　hate　you　　the　whole __ night __ through　　in -

stead　of　hav - ing　sweet　dreams __ a - bout　you.

you.

SWINGIN'

Words and Music by JOHN DAVID ANDERSON
and LIONEL DELMORE

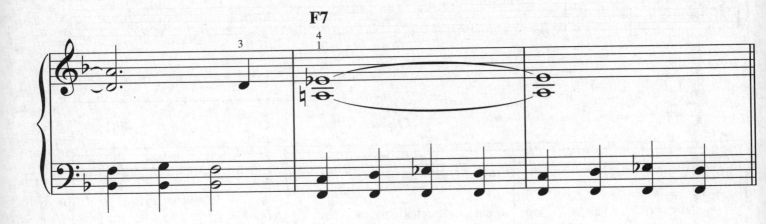

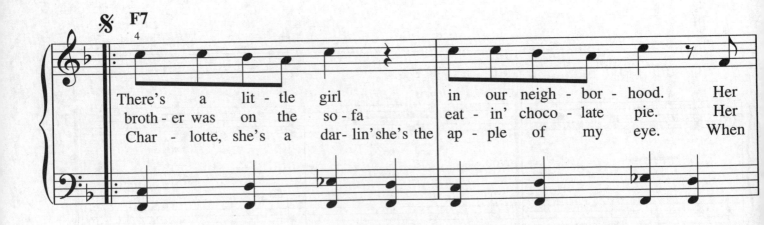

There's a lit-tle girl in our neigh-bor-hood. Her
broth-er was on the so-fa eat-in' choco-late pie. Her
Char-lotte, she's a dar-lin' she's the ap-ple of my eye. When

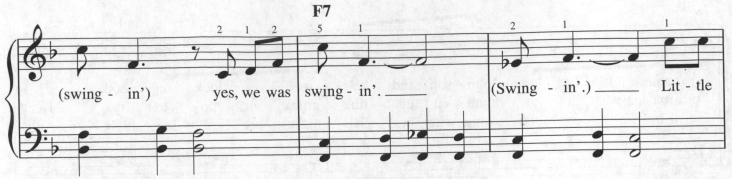

(swing - in') yes, we was swing - in'. _____ (Swing - in'.) _____ Lit - tle

Char - lotte, she's as pret - ty as the an - gels when they sing. _____ I

can't be - lieve I'm out here on her front porch in the swing, just a

To Coda ⊕   **D.S. al Coda**

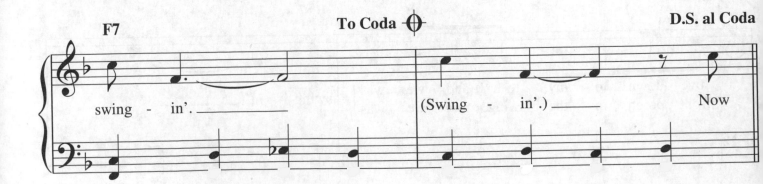

swing - in'. _____ (Swing - in'.) _____ Now

CODA

F7   **C7**

(Swing - in'.) Lit - tle Char - lotte, she's as pret - ty as the

B7   **B♭7**

an - gels when they sing.___ I can't be - lieve I'm out here on her

F7

front porch in the swing, just a swing - in'.___

(Swing - in'.)___

TENNESSEE WALTZ

Words and Music by REDD STEWART
and PEE WEE KING

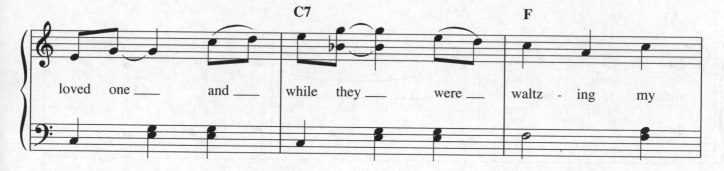

loved one ___ and ___ while they ___ were ___ waltz - ing my

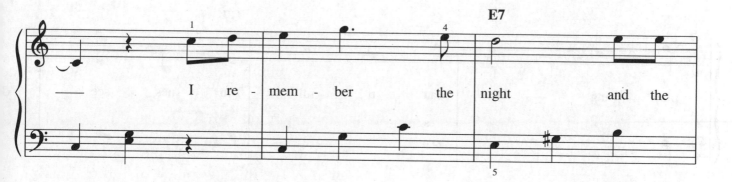

friend stole my sweet - heart from me. ___

___ I re - mem - ber the night and the

Ten - nes - see Waltz. Now I know just how

A7   **D7**   **G7**

much   I   have   lost. _____   Yes,   I

C   **C7**

lost   my ___   lit - tle   dar - lin' ___   the ___   night   they ___   were ___

F   **C**   **G7**

play - ing   the   beau - ti - ful   Ten - nes - see

1. **C**   **2.** **C**

Waltz. _____   I was   Waltz.

rit.

THEN

Words and Music by ASHLEY GORLEY,
BRAD PAISLEY and CHRIS DUBOIS

Moderately

I re-mem-ber   try-in' not to stare   the night that I   first
I re-mem-ber   tak-in' you __ back   to right where I   first

met you.   You had me mes-mer-ized. __   And
met you.   You were so sur-prised.   There were

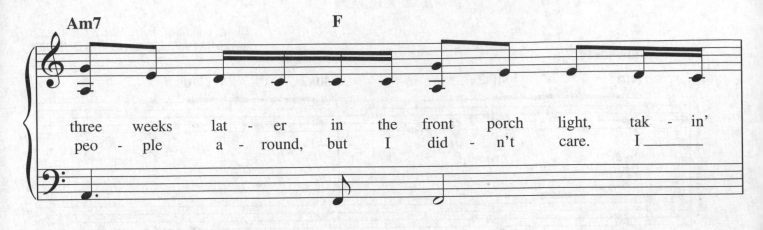

three weeks lat - er in the front porch light, tak - in'
peo - ple a - round, but I did - n't care. I

for - ty - five min - utes to kiss good - night. I had - n't
got down on one knee right there and

F   F   G

told you yet, but I thought I loved you then.
once a - gain, I thought I loved you then.

And now you're my whole life,
But now you're my whole life,
And now you're my whole life, now you're my whole

world, and I just can't _ be - lieve the way I feel a - bout _ you

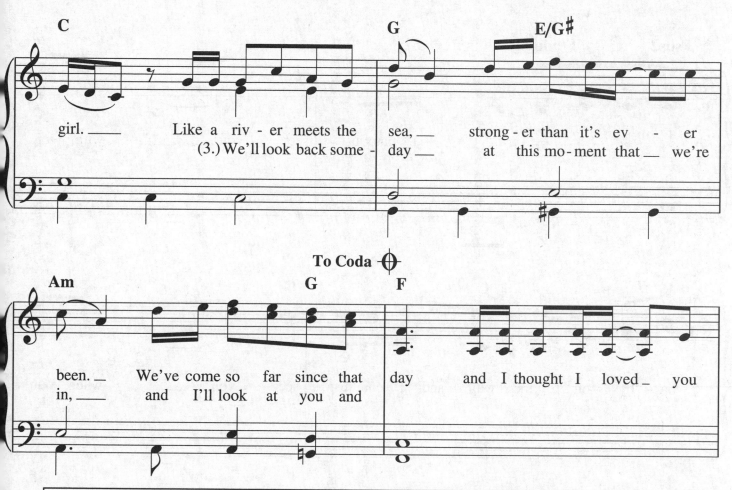

girl. ___ Like a riv - er meets the sea, ___ strong - er than it's ev - er
(3.) We'll look back some - day ___ at this mo - ment that _ we're

To Coda ⊕

been. _ We've come so far since that day and I thought I loved _ you
in, ___ and I'll look at you and

1.

then.

2.

then. _____

I can just see you _____ with a

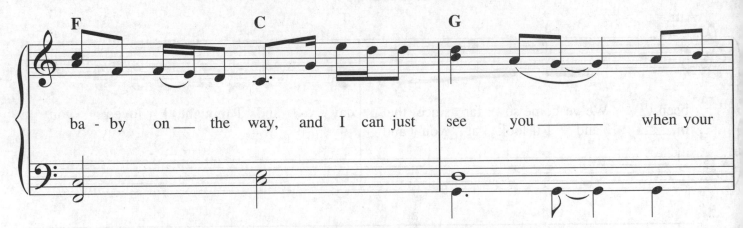

ba - by on __ the way, and I can just see you _____ when your

hair is turn - in' gray. What I can't see is how I'm ev - er gon - na love you

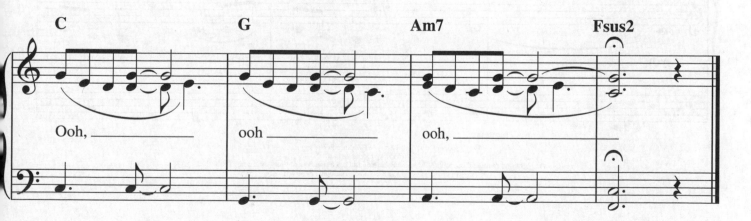

WALKIN' AFTER MIDNIGHT

Lyrics by DON HECHT
Music by ALAN W. BLOCK

I go out

walk-in' ___ af - ter mid - night ___ in ___ the moon-light ___ just

like we used to do. I'm al-ways walk-in' ___ af - ter mid-night ___ search - in' for

you. ___ I walk for miles ___ a - long the

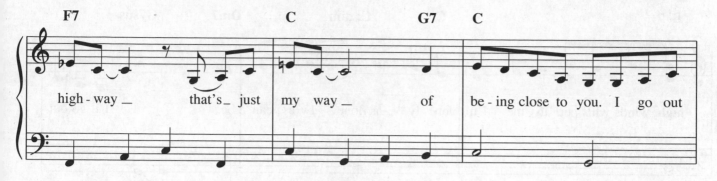

high-way __ that's_ just my way __ of be-ing close to you. I go out

walk-in' __ af-ter mid-night_ search-in' for you.

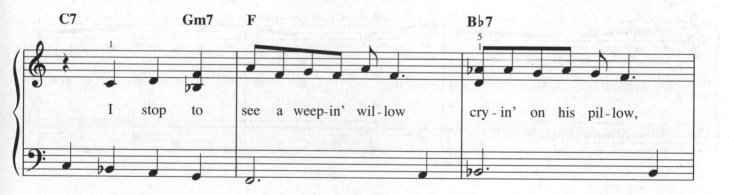

I stop to see a weep-in' wil-low cry-in' on his pil-low,

may-be he's cry-in' for me. And as the sky turns gloom-y,

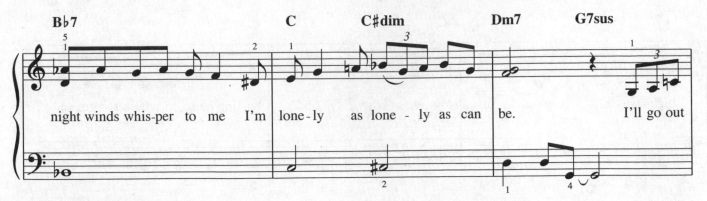

B♭7

night winds whis-per to me I'm lone-ly as lone-ly as can be.

I'll go out

C   **C♯dim**   **Dm7**   **G7sus**

C   **F7**   **C**   **G7**

walk-in' ___ af - ter mid - night ___ in ___ the star - light ___ and

C   **F7**

pray that you may be some-where just walk-in' ___ af - ter mid-night ___ search - in' for

1.
C   **F**   **C**   **G7sus**

2.
C   **F**   **C**

me. ___ I go out me.

WELCOME TO MY WORLD

Words and Music by RAY WINKLER
and JOHN HATHCOCK

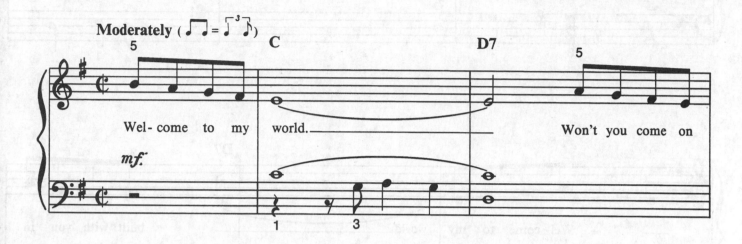

Wel- come to my world._____ Won't you come on

in?_____ Mir- a- cles, I guess, still

still hap- pen now and then._____ Step in- to my

heart; _____ Leave your cares be - hind. _____

_____ Wel- come to my world _____ built with you in

mind. _____ Knock and the door _____ will

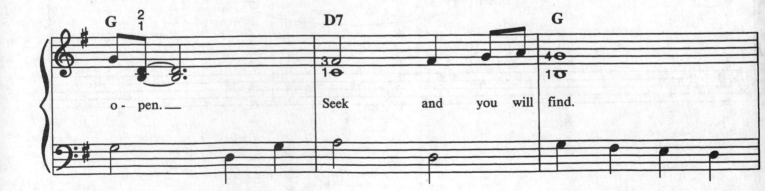

o - pen. _____ Seek and you will find.

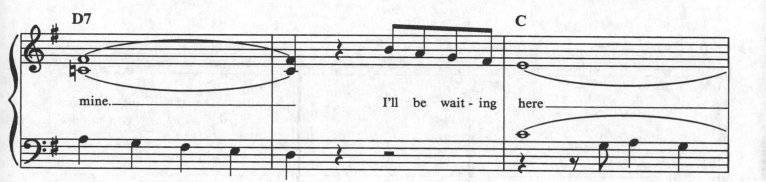

WHEN YOU SAY NOTHING AT ALL

Words and Music by DON SCHLITZ
and PAUL OVERSTREET

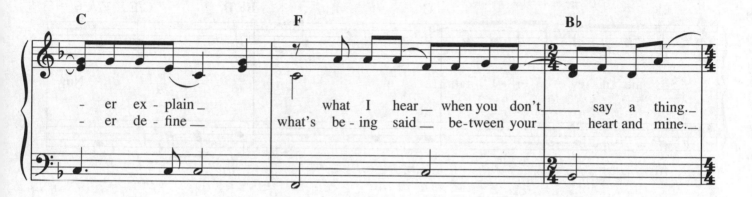

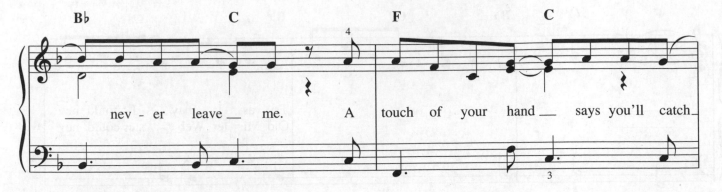

B♭ **C** **F** **C**

never leave me. A touch of your hand says you'll catch

B♭ **C** **B♭/D** **C/E** **F/A**

me if ev-er I fall. Now

B♭ To Coda **C** **F** **C**

you say it best when you say noth-ing at all.

B♭ **C** **F** **C/E** **B/D** **C**

2.
C   F   C

when you say noth - ing at all.

Bb   C   F   C   Bb   D.S. al Coda

The

CODA
C   F   C   Bb   C

when you say noth-ing at   all.

F   C/E   Bb/D   Csus   F

WHY ME?
(Why Me, Lord?)

Words and Music by
KRIS KRISTOFFERSON

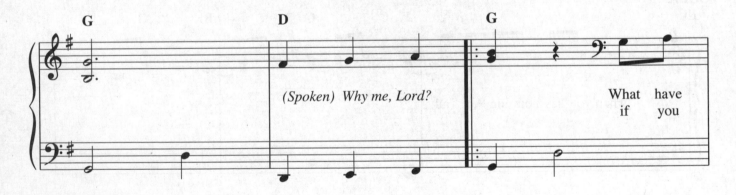

(Spoken) Why me, Lord?

What have
if you

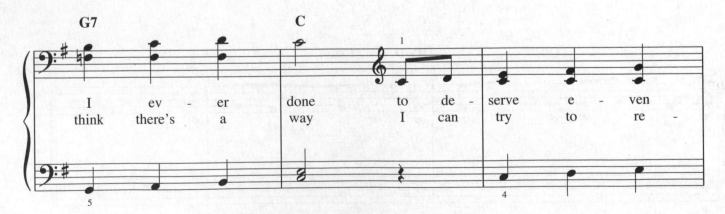

I ev - er
think there's a

done
way

to de -
I can

serve
try

e -
to

ven
re -

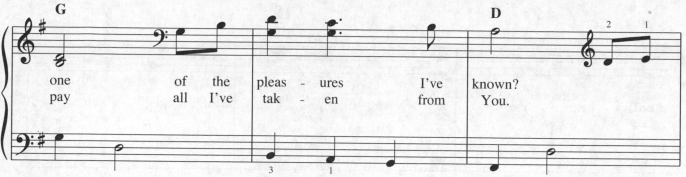

one   of   the   pleas - ures   I've   known?
pay   all   I've   tak - en   from   You.

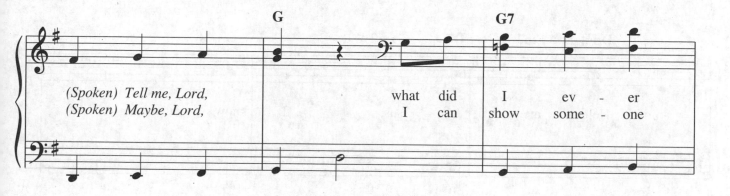

(Spoken) Tell me, Lord,   what   did   I   ev - er
(Spoken) Maybe, Lord,   I   can   show   some - one

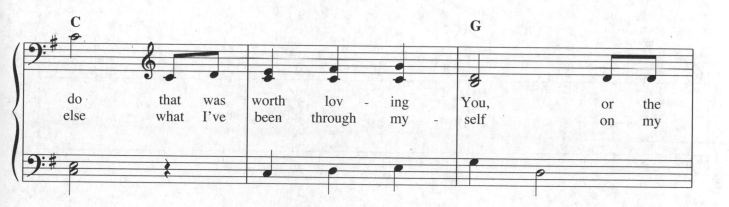

do   that   was   worth   lov - ing   You,   or   the
else   what   I've   been   through   my - self   on   my

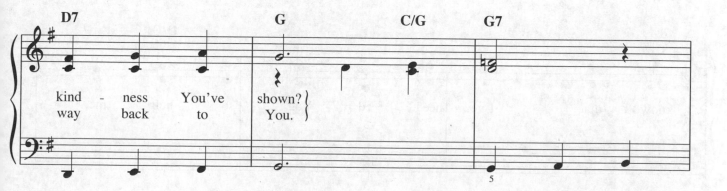

kind - ness   You've   shown?
way   back   to   You.

Lord, help me, Je - sus, I've wast - ed it

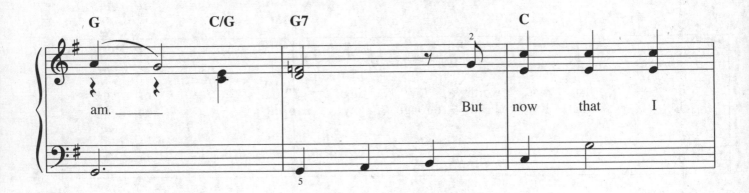

so. Help me, Je - sus; I know what I

am. _____ But now that I

know that I've need - ed You so, help me,

Je - sus; my soul's in Your hands.

To Coda ⊕ **G**

1.

D   **2.** **G**   **C/G**   **G7**   **D.S. al Coda**

(Spoken) Try me, Lord,   hands.

CODA

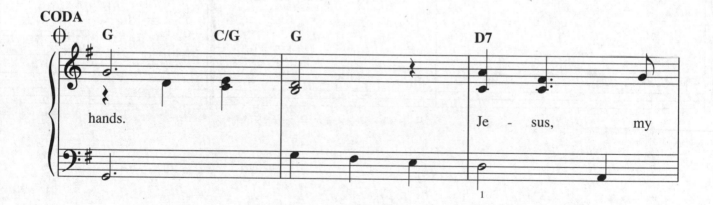

⊕ **G**   **C/G**   **G**   **D7**

hands.   Je - sus,   my

C   **G/B**   **Am7**   **G**

soul's in Your hands.
rit.

YOU ARE MY SUNSHINE

Words and Music by
JIMMIE DAVIS

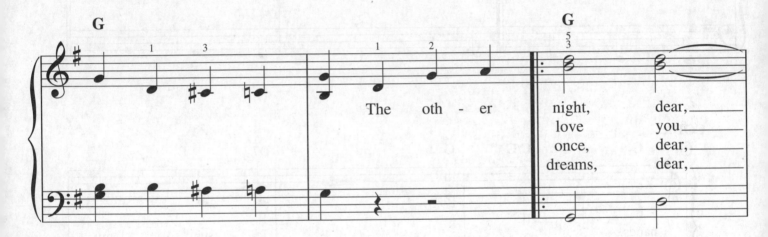

The oth-er
love
once,
dreams,

night, dear,_____
you_____
dear,_____
dear,_____

_____ as I lay_____ sleep - ing_____ I dreamed I
_____ and make you_____ hap - py_____ if you will
_____ you real - ly_____ loved me_____ and no
_____ you seem to_____ leave me._____ When I a -

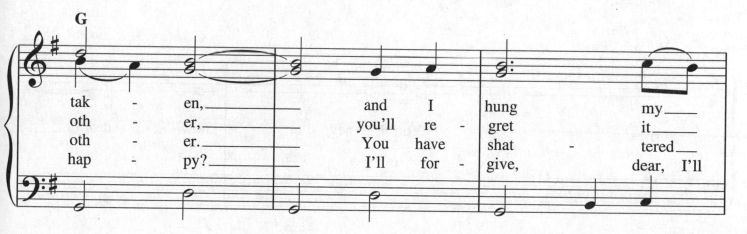

sun - shine, _____ my on - ly _____ sun - shine. _____

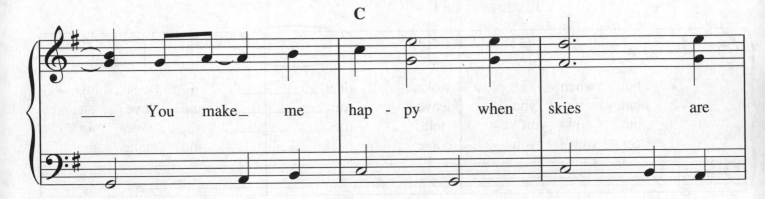

_____ You make __ me hap - py when skies are

gray. You'll nev - er know, dear, _____

_____ how much I love _____ you. _____ Please don't

take my — sun - shine a - way.

I'll al - ways
You told me
In all my

YOU HAD ME FROM HELLO

Words and Music by SKIP EWING
and KENNY CHESNEY

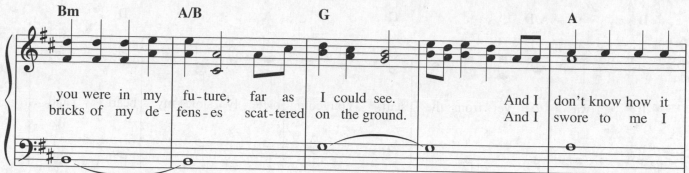

Bm / A/B / G / A

you were in my fu-ture, far as I could see. And I don't know how it
bricks of my de-fens-es scat-tered on the ground. And I swore to me I

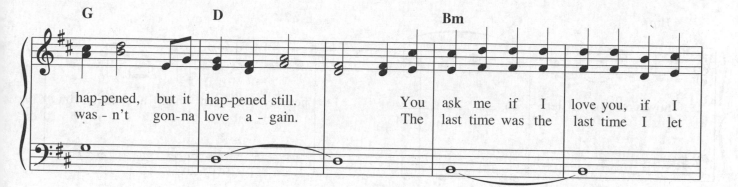

G / D / Bm

hap-pened, but it hap-pened still. You ask me if I love you, if I
was-n't gon-na love a-gain. The last time was the last time I let

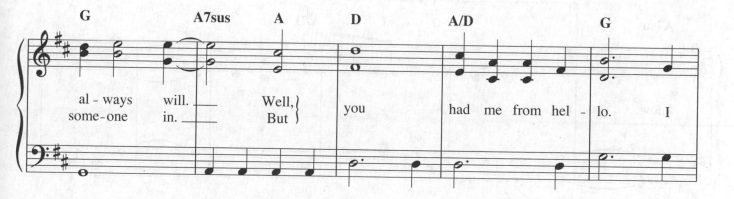

G / A7sus / A / D / A/D / G

al-ways will. ___ Well, you had me from hel-lo. I
some-one in. ___ But

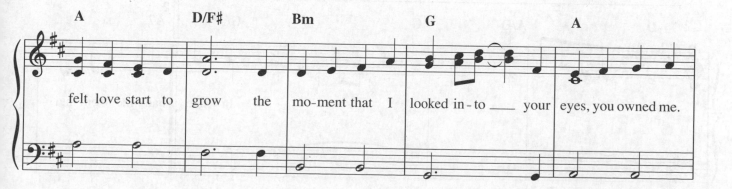

A / D/F♯ / Bm / G / A

felt love start to grow the mo-ment that I looked in-to ___ your eyes, you owned me.

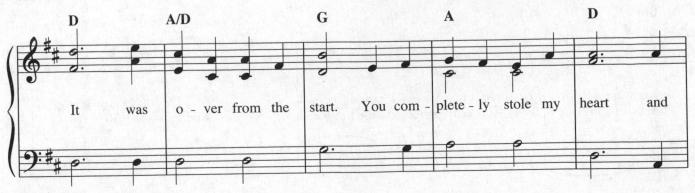

It was o - ver from the start. You com - plete - ly stole my heart and

now you won't _ let go. _____ I nev - er e - ven had a chance, you

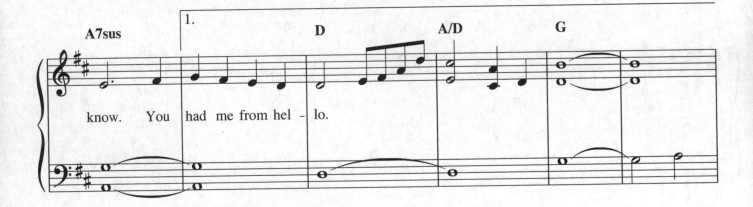

know. You had me from hel - lo.

In - side had me from hel -

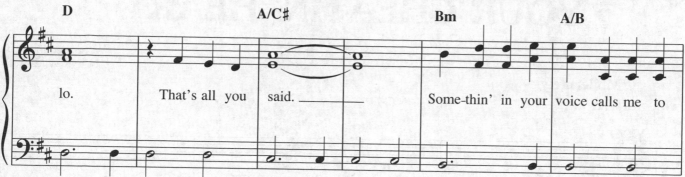

lo.　　　That's all you　said. 　　　　Some-thin' in your voice calls me to

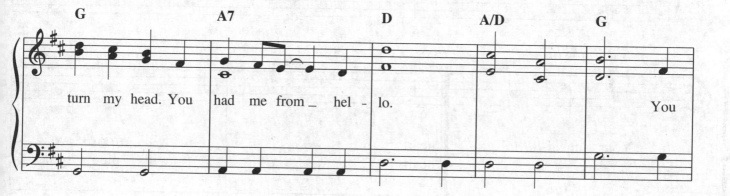

turn my head. You　had me from _ hel - lo.　　　　You

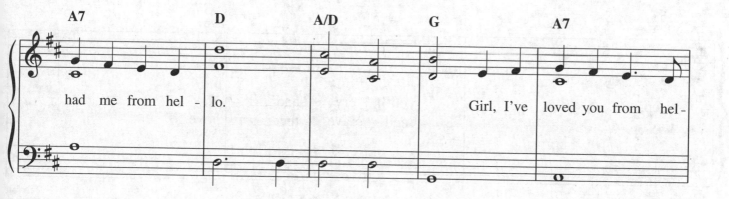

had me from hel - lo.　　　　　Girl, I've　loved you from　hel-

lo.

YOUR CHEATIN' HEART

Words and Music by
HANK WILLIAMS

and call my name._____ You'll walk the___

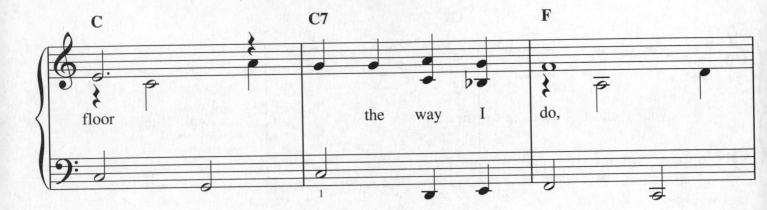

floor the way I do,

your cheat - in'___ heart will tell on

1.
you. Your cheat - in'___ you.
2.